INTELLECTUAL PROPERTY AND THE BRAIN

Although legal scholars have begun to explore the implications of neuroscientific research for criminal law, the field has yet to assess the potential of such research for intellectual property law – a legal regime governing over one-third of the US economy. *Intellectual Property and the Brain* addresses this gap by showing how tools meant to improve our understanding of human behavior inevitably shape the balance of power between artists and copyists, businesses and consumers. This first of its kind book demonstrates how neuroscience can improve our flawed approach to regulating creative conduct and commercial communications when applied with careful attention to the reasons that our system of intellectual property law exists. With a host of real-life examples of art, design, and advertising, the book charts a path forward for legal actors seeking reforms that will unlock artistic innovation, elevate economic productivity, and promote consumer welfare.

Mark Bartholomew is a full professor at the University at Buffalo School of Law, where he teaches and writes in the areas of intellectual property and law and technology, with an emphasis on copyright law, trademark law, advertising regulation, and online privacy. He is the author of *Adcreep: The Case Against Modern Marketing* (2017).

Intellectual Property and the Brain

HOW NEUROSCIENCE WILL RESHAPE LEGAL PROTECTION FOR CREATIONS OF THE MIND

Mark Bartholomew

University at Buffalo School of Law

CAMBRIDGE
UNIVERSITY PRESS

CAMBRIDGE
UNIVERSITY PRESS

University Printing House, Cambridge CB2 8BS, United Kingdom

One Liberty Plaza, 20th Floor, New York, NY 10006, USA

477 Williamstown Road, Port Melbourne, VIC 3207, Australia

314–321, 3rd Floor, Plot 3, Splendor Forum, Jasola District Centre, NewDelhi – 110025, India

103 Penang Road, #05–06/07, Visioncrest Commercial, Singapore 238467

Cambridge University Press is part of the University of Cambridge.

It furthers the University's mission by disseminating knowledge in the pursuit of education, learning, and research at the highest international levels of excellence.

www.cambridge.org
Information on this title: www.cambridge.org/9781009189569
DOI: 10.1017/9781009189545

First published 2022

A catalogue record for this publication is available from the British Library.

Library of Congress Cataloging-in-Publication Data
Names: Bartholomew, Mark, 1971- author.
Title: Intellectual property and the brain : how neuroscience will reshape legal protection for creations of the mind / Mark Bartholomew, University at Buffalo School of Law.
Description: Cambridge, United Kingdom ; New York, NY : Cambridge University Press, 2022. | Includes bibliographical references and index.
Identifiers: LCCN 2022001114 (print) | LCCN 2022001115 (ebook) | ISBN 9781009189569 (hardback) | ISBN 9781009189552 (paperback) | ISBN 9781009189545 (epub)
Subjects: LCSH: Intellectual property–United States. | Copyright–United States. | Copyright infringement–United States. | Neurosciences–Law and legislation–United States. | Law–Psychological aspects.
Classification: LCC KF2979 .B39 2022 (print) | LCC KF2979 (ebook) | DDC 346.7304/8–dc23/eng/20220429
LC record available at https://lccn.loc.gov/2022001114
LC ebook record available at https://lccn.loc.gov/2022001115

ISBN 978-1-009-18956-9 Hardback
ISBN 978-1-009-18955-2 Paperback

CONTENTS

LIST OF FIGURES

ACKNOWLEDGMENTS

Many, many people helped me better understand the intersection of intellectual property law and brain science. There is not enough room here to name them all, but I would like to single out Pete Alces, Samuel Becher, Michael Boucai, Sarah Burstein, Anjan Chatterjee, Shubha Ghosh, Ming Hsu, Joyce Lacey, Mike Madison, John Monahan, Francis Shen, Brian Soucek, Chris Sprigman, and John Tehranian.

These folks all provided invaluable feedback either on this book or on earlier work on which this book relies. The same goes for Christine, Clara, and Hank Bartholomew, who not only provided suggestions responsible for markedly improving the final product but also gave their love and support when my own brain found itself overtaxed in trying to understand the brains of others. Of course, all errors and oversights are mine alone.

Portions of this book were adapted from parts of the following articles: "Copyright and the Brain," *Washington University Law Review* 98 (2020): 525–86; "Copyright and the Creative Process," *Notre Dame Law Review* 97 (2021): 357–416; and "Neuromarks," *Minnesota Law Review* 103 (2018): 521–85. For a more in-depth treatment of some of the design patent issues discussed here, see "Nonobvious Design," *Iowa Law Review* 108 (forthcoming 2022).

ACKNOWLEDGEMENTS

INTRODUCTION

The fortunes of over one-third of the economy of the United States – nearly seven trillion dollars – depend on two kinds of people. The first kind of person makes a strong impression. She turns heads with her "true artistic skill" and "creative judgment." She is "original." Members of this exclusive group are not always humble, probably because their behavior is celebrated as reflecting "genius" or "magic."

The second kind of person is someone you would likely not even notice if you saw them at a party or walking down the street. Unlike the first person, this person is thoroughly conventional. Her musical tastes are "average," her design preferences "ordinary." Her attention to commercial messaging is "typical" and "unheeding." Rather than being characterized as a genius, this person has been called "ignorant," "gullible," and, in particularly uncharitable moments, "a moron in a hurry."

The first person I am describing is a creator, as defined by the laws of intellectual property. Copyright protection is reserved for authors possessing a "creative spark." Commercial designers can only claim patent rights when their output is "nonobvious" and "inventive." The second person is the average audience member. It is this person's reactions to art, design, and advertising that determine the metes and bounds of intellectual property protection. In this way, the first person is always at the mercy of the second.

Every legal dispute involving an assertion of copyright, patent, or trademark rights demands some investigation of the thought processes of creators and the audiences for their creations. Yet despite their centrality to intellectual property law, these two kinds of people are not well understood by Congress or the courts. A perennial complaint from judges deciding intellectual property disputes is that they lack the tools to comprehend the minds of artists and inventors. "[J]udges can make fools of themselves pronouncing on aesthetic matters," warns one leading legal jurist.[1] Similar concerns apply to efforts to understand the thoughts and feelings of audiences. As one judge fatalistically described it, "[a]fter 200 years of wrestling with copyright questions," the legal system has not come up with a way to understand how the average observer or listener will compare two artistic works in her head and "it is unlikely that courts will come up with the answer any time soon."[2]

What if there was an answer, a way to understand the thought processes of these two groups of people? We tend to think of neuroscientists as working to find causes and cures of neurodegenerative ailments like Alzheimer's and Parkinson's disease, but this represents only a tiny fraction of neuroscientific research. Scientists track changes in blood flow and oxygenation in the brain to discover how our minds appreciate "beauty" in literature. They identify different neural signatures that reveal not only when someone is thinking of one brand or another – Coke or Pepsi, BMW or Audi – but also the success of corporate advertising in communicating desirable brand attributes like ruggedness or sophistication. Researchers record fleeting electrical impulses signifying whether an observer considers two separate objects to be closely related or far apart. In other words, neuroscience now offers probative information on the very thought processes that have long bedeviled judges and juries. It is time to see how our new appreciation of the biology of human thought can shed light on intellectual property – the legal regime governing the movies we see, the music we listen to, the computers we use, the clothes we wear, and so much more.

INTELLECTUAL PROPERTY'S BRAIN FREEZE

Whether we realize it or not, intellectual property – a term referring to the use or value of ideas rather than tangible items – is an ever-present force in our lives.[3] Think of how you interact with your phone, a consumer product the average American checks over one hundred times a day. The facial recognition technology that unlocks your phone is the subject of a patent as is the phone's overall look. The songs streamed from your phone are governed by copyright law. Any aspect of your phone that is attached in the public's mind to a particular source – from the icons it displays to the Apple logo to the Samsung name – are protected from imitation by trademark law. Of course, it is not just your phone. Intellectual property law applies to much if not most of the communications we make and receive, the consumer products we buy, and the cultural artifacts we experience and share.

Intellectual property law grants limited ownership in inventions and creative expression to spur innovation and to protect consumers from marketplace deception. The Founding Fathers thought the subject of intellectual property important enough to explicitly provide for systems of copyright and patent protection in the text of the US Constitution. As manufacturing's role in the economy dwindled, intellectual property rose to become "a primary driver of US economic growth and national competitiveness."[4] Intellectual property law is also of central cultural significance, its rules influencing what expressive products come to market and what raw materials can and cannot be repurposed for subsequent creations.

Despite its economic and cultural importance, intellectual property law is plagued by unpredictable and unspecified legal tests. Businesses trying to safeguard their brands – often their most valuable asset – have to trust in a judge's best guess as to the brand's signaling power, emotional aura, and resemblance to other brands rather than any reliable estimate of consumer perception. The task of any artist arguing infringement of their art, from songwriters to sculptors, is to convince a judge or jury that audiences will consider the defendant's work as similar to their own without any meaningful definition of what "similar" means. To be eligible for copyright protection, an expressive work must be creative, but courts are so skeptical of their own ability to discern creativity that this legal requirement is only enforced sporadically.

Granted, it is difficult to specify most legal tests with absolute precision.[5] Nevertheless, from crimes to contracts, other areas of the law manage to interrogate the mental states of others with less consternation. There are a few reasons courts have found the psychological condition of artists and audiences so difficult to decipher. The subject matter of copyright as well as a growing portion of patent law implicates aesthetic judgment, which judges have long believed not susceptible to reasoned deliberation. In fact, in the law of intellectual property, there is inscribed a deep double standard. Scientific creations are compared against other inventions to determine if they are sufficiently innovative whereas artistic creations are considered impossible to compare against anything else given the mysteries of the creative process. Judges also fear charges of cultural elitism. Rather than risk being labeled out of touch with the sentiments of ordinary purchasers and audiences, they continue to apply amorphous tests for determining when one trademark, creative work, or product design should be deemed too close to another.

Regardless of the reasons for it, all this legal uncertainty is problematic. Designers find themselves targets of cease and desist letters merely for using common geometric shapes. Without more clarity, artists cannot be certain that their projects will be protected from copyists and fraudsters or that their creative efforts will not be embargoed for resembling a past work. The tens of millions spent to launch a new brand may rest on a judge's "shaky kind of guess" as to whether consumers will be confused by another party's somewhat similar trade symbol.[6] Sometimes the judge or jury will ultimately arrive at what is arguably the right assessment of creator and audience states of mind. Even so, all the ambiguity surrounding these determinations prevents cases from being decided quickly, generating significant legal fees and opening up creators and businesses to extortionate demands. Recent advances in the measurement of human thought promise a dose of clarity for the uncertainty that has paralyzed the law of intellectual property for decades.

NEUROSCIENTIFIC PROMISES AND PITFALLS

Thanks to machines that can reveal neural processes as they happen, researchers now have a ringside seat to the biological mechanisms evident in different kinds of thought processes. Functional magnetic resonance imaging (fMRI) scanners record fluctuations in brain blood flow and oxygenation, thereby revealing which areas of the brain are activated by particular stimuli. Devices for detecting the electric and magnetic fields associated with neural activity in the brain – the most important of which is electroencephalography (EEG) – have been around for years, but have recently become vastly more valuable thanks to greater processing speeds that can measure the rapid neural changes that mark cognitive and emotional response. These processing speeds allow researchers to compare shifts in neurological function mere milliseconds apart. Most importantly, these technologies provide a way to understand mental activity without relying on an individual's problematic attempts to identify and describe their inner thoughts to others.

This is not to say that EEG and fMRI data can reveal all or even most of the brain's secrets. In addition to the brain being incredibly complex, there is a certain amount of subjectivity in the reading of brain scans; it is not always clear how an influx of blood or electrical impulses to a particular neural territory should be interpreted. With this kind of research, there is always the danger of reverse inference – crediting neural activation to a particular cognitive process instead of acknowledging that multiple processes could prompt the same activation. EEG research lacks the ability to track the precise contours of brain activity whereas fMRI imaging suffers from temporal restrictions.

Neuroscientists recognize these problems. They adjust their methodology and conclusions in light of the dangers of reverse inference. They test for multiregional brain activity rather than only looking for activity in a single area. They combine fMRI and EEG measurements to achieve maximal spatial and temporal resolution.[7] Neuroscience's limitations counsel caution, but not willfull ignorance of its revelations about how our minds work.

It is also important to admit that, at this stage, neuroscience cannot reliably tell us what one single creator, designer, audience member, or consumer is thinking. Most neuroscientific research involves the aggregation of many brain scans, not the neural portrait of a single person. Given human variability, using data from a group of test subjects to explain the mental behavior of a single individual lacks sufficient reliability. Legal scholars label this this the "G2i" problem.[8]

But this limitation is actually what makes intellectual property law such an attractive terrain for neuroscientific input. Even though criminal law has attracted the lion's share of attention from members of the legal academy eager to apply neuroscientific insights, its focus on a single defendant's mental state at the time of offense makes brain scan data of limited value. Unlike criminal law, intellectual property law relies on information about aggregate thought processes, not the thought processes of an individual. According to the statutes governing copyright, patent, and trademark law and the cases interpreting them, it is this aggregate sense of how most artists create and most audience members see and hear that determines whether or not a work is protectable or infringement has taken place. Because it does not have to confront the G2i obstacles involved with pinpointing one person's legally determinative mental state, intellectual property law is better suited to benefit from neuroscientific research than other legal subject areas.

PSYCHOLOGY AND THE LAW'S MIXED TRACK RECORD

Some reading this may remain skeptical of neuroscience's promise, questioning how biological records can offer real insight into the laws governing artistic expression and consumer behavior. In the pages that follow, I describe a growing body of reliable and probative evidence of the mental operations of creators and audiences. Neuroscience has already left its mark on many areas of the law outside of intellectual property. Between 2005 and 2015, over 2800 judicial opinions were published involving neuroscientific evidence submitted by defendants.[9] Thanks to proof of the plasticity of the developing brain, some criminal punishments for juvenile offenders are no longer allowed.[10] The vast field of tort law now takes fMRI imaging into account; such images were credited with forcing the National Football League into a settlement with thousands of former players suffering from Chronic Traumatic Encephalopathy. It stands to reason that the modern revolution in brain science is likely to influence intellectual property law, just as it has these other legal subject matters.

Even if you remain doubtful, there is still good reason to begin the analytical groundwork for brain imaging's relationship to intellectual property law. Courts sometimes embrace scientific evidence that turns out to have limited empirical validity. In one notorious episode, psychologists provided important professional and academic cover for a series of eugenics laws in the early twentieth century, resulting in the forced sterilization of between sixty and seventy thousand people.[11] Moreover, once a new technology for observing human behavior secures a place in legal doctrine or practice, it can become impossible to displace. For example, despite the demonstrated unreliability of much of forensic science, including ballistics tests and the matching of latent fingerprints, such evidence has become a bedrock of the American criminal justice system.[12] The history of law and psychology suggests that even if some concerns remain about the accuracy of neuroscientific records of creators and their audiences, these concerns may not prevent their use to decide intellectual property disputes.

At the same time, neuroscience is unlikely to completely displace longstanding methods for deciding intellectual property disputes. Predictions of a criminal law neurorevolution, where brain science would "transform[] people's moral intuitions about free will and responsibility" simply have not come to pass.[13] To the contrary, the legal concepts of causation, responsibility, and blame rely on a default understanding of human behavior that is largely autonomous and resistant to outside forces. Despite years of psychological research (including neuroscientific research) pushing against this understanding of human behavior, those concepts remain firmly in place.

Neuroscience's important but limited influence on criminal law is evidence of a larger phenomenon. However compelling, psychological insights typically do not replace wholesale the established prerogatives of judges and juries. Although law is fundamentally concerned with human behavior and neuroscience is changing our view of human behavior, ultimately legal precepts involve value judgments that are rarely shaken by scientific evidence, no matter how empirically robust. The author of a comprehensive analysis of legislation shaped by neuroscience finds that "[n]euroscience is typically embraced when it affirms, rather than challenges, preexisting normative commitments."[14] Or, as put colorfully by one psychologist and legal scholar about the use of psychological evidence more generally, "The law uses psychology like a drunk uses a lamp post – more for support than illumination."[15] Predictions of neuroscience's transformative impact on the law need to be leavened by an appreciation of the fundamentally conservative nature of legal change.

But if neuroscience will not revolutionize intellectual property law, it will shape it in significant albeit contained ways. Deeply held values – like the criminal justice system's focus on individual blame – will likely always withstand assault from psychological evidence to the contrary. At the same time, well-known factual propositions like the unreliability of hearsay evidence have no need for bolstering from psychological study. In between these two poles lies the area where insights into human behavior can reshape the law. The legal scholar Harry Kalven speculated that social science influences the law in "a middle range" "where the premises are not that unshakeable and where the facts are not that accessible."[16] Changes to this middle area do not threaten to topple fundamental pillars of the legal system. Because their effects are limited in scope, such changes are also less threatening to judicial prerogatives and more likely to be welcomed. It is the goal of this book to describe what is probable when it comes to the intersection of neuroscience and intellectual property law, not impossible, by mapping out this middle range of scientific and legal possibility.

CHARTING INTELLECTUAL PROPERTY LAW'S NEURAL TURN

Given its influence on other areas of the law and the amount of academic and applied research being conducted on questions of creativity, artistic appreciation, and consumer perception, neuroscientific evidence will likely work its way into specific pockets of intellectual property law. It will reconfigure some tests based on judicial intuition but without toppling the entire system. Some of these alterations will be beneficial, but, given the mistakes of the past, others will not and must be guarded against. The normative principles animating intellectual property law need to be kept in mind lest neuroscience's new estimates of human thought lead to suboptimal outcomes for consumer protection or artistic freedom. My aim here is offer a template for marrying the science with the law in a way that stays true to those principles.

The remainder of this book is divided into three parts. The first describes how both copyright and patent law hinge on best guesses about the creative process and how neuroscientific insights could improve this guesswork. Chapter 1 compares copyright law's understanding of creativity with brain science's revelations about the creative process. In 1903, in one of his most influential opinions, Oliver Wendell Holmes warned that it would be "a dangerous undertaking" for judges to try to understand the thought processes of artists.[17] Following Holmes, modern judges have turned the creativity requirement into a test that everyone passes, generating a flood of copyrightable output that citizens unknowingly interact with and (illegally) copy from every day. Neuroscientific studies of the creative process reveal that artistic ingenuity is not the black box the law supposes it to be, exploding several popular myths about art and artists – myths that judges since Holmes have used to rationalize their failure to truly interrogate creativity.

Chapter 2 turns to design patents. Once a sleepy backwater of intellectual property law, design patent filings skyrocketed after a half-a-billion-dollar verdict for a patentee in 2012. In determining whether a design warrants patent protection, judges refuse to consider any single design element's salience to consumers or other designers, reasoning that the design process is so personal and subjective that they lack the understanding needed to elevate one design feature over another. This stands in sharp contrast to the law's assumptions about scientific invention, which permits objective and focused evaluation of the invention against its prior art. This art/science double standard does not jibe with evidence that, for scientists as well as designers, both sides of the brain must be engaged in the same process: coming up with an idea, then building on that idea so that it is useful.

The book's second part examines how audiences perceive artistic and commercial stimuli, contrasting the science with the legal tests for copyright, patent, and trademark infringement. Chapter 3 turns to copyright law's test for infringement, which asks a court or jury to assess whether the parties' works are "substantially similar" from the vantage point of the "ordinary observer." Embedded within this test are several assumptions about audiences and art that "neuroaesthetics" – the study of the neural processes underlying aesthetic behavior – calls into question, chief among them that we all appreciate works in the same indescribable way and that one juror or judge's reaction is as good as another. In truth, the basic biology of aesthetic reaction changes markedly depending on familiarity, experience, and even gender, contradicting copyright law's one size-fits-all-approach.

Visual processing is arguably the best understood mental process in modern neuroscience, shedding light on the mechanics of design perception and appreciation. Chapter 4 describes recent studies showing that aesthetic preference is strongly tied to the ease with which an observer can mentally process a particular design. Although a limited amount of innovation may be needed to gain the observer's attention, consumers insist on simplicity, familiarity, and congruence in designs. Design patent law presumes that consumers prefer visually innovative products but, in reality, innovation in design, after rapidly reaching an optimal level, begins to trigger aesthetic distaste.

Chapter 5 explores the burgeoning field of consumer neuroscience. Neuroscientists contend that each trademark has a different neural signature, with different brain regions reflecting perceptions like "excitement," "ruggedness," or "sophistication" upon exposure to the brand stimulus. By viewing these neural signatures and nothing else, researchers could distinguish whether the subject was thinking about Apple or Microsoft, Gucci or Louis Vuitton, hinting at a future where fMRI readings replace today's judicial guesswork about when consumers will mistake one trademark for another.

The book's final part consists of three chapters prescribing how lawyers and judges can utilize neuroscientific insights to improve the law of intellectual property. To better diagnose a work's creativity, Chapter 6 urges courts to investigate authorial motivations, solicit the input of experts in the field, and privilege design choices rendering a design harder to visually process. These changes would bolster the law's role in incentivizing the production of creative works while avoiding awards of copyright and patent to unoriginal works that can stymie downstream innovation. Chapter 7 describes how the test for copyright infringement may be altered to take differences in audiences and artistic media into account. Chapter 8 argues that even though neuroscience offers windows into two kinds of consumer reasoning – a deliberative, cognitive mode and an automatic, emotional mode – courts should avoid using evidence of the latter to extend trademark law to legally prevent changes in a brand's emotional meaning.

This final part also responds to concerns that neuroscience could do violence to the humanistic values and other ideals currently embedded in the structures of copyright, patent, and trademark law. Studies reveal that neuroscientific research can sometimes be too persuasive, raising fears that attorneys will use colorful pictures of the brain to convince legal decision-makers of unproven phenomena.[18] Neuroscience can offer much to improve our flawed system for regulating creative conduct and commercial communications, but it needs to be applied judiciously and with attention to the reasons our system of intellectual property exists in the first place.

Notes

[1]   Gracen v. Bradford Exch., 698 F.2d 300, 304 (7th Cir. 1983).

[2]   Nash v. CBS, Inc., 899 F.2d 1537, 1540 (7th Cir. 1990).

[3]   Justin Hughes, *The Philosophy of Intellectual Property*, 77 GEO. L.J. 287, 294 (1988).

[4]   Economics and Statistics Administration and U.S. Patent and Trademark Office, Intellectual Property and the U.S. Economy: Industries in Focus (Mar. 2012), https://www.uspto.gov/sites/default/files/news/publications/IP_Report_March_2012.pdf.

[5]   There is a wealth of legal scholarship discussing whether a law should be given content ex ante as in a "rule" or ex post as with a "standard." See Louis Kaplow, *Rules versus Standards: An Economic Analysis*, 42 DUKE L.J. 557 (1992).

[6]   Triangle Publ'ns v. Rohrlich, 167 F.2d 969, 976 (2d Cir. 1948).

[7]   See, for example, Stefan Debener et al., *Single-Trial EEG-fMRI Reveals the Dynamics of Cognitive Function*, 10 TRENDS COGNITIVE SCI. 558, 558 (2006).

[8]   David L. Faigman et al., *Group to Individual (G2i) Inference in Scientific Expert Testimony*, 81 U. CHI. L. REV. 417 (2014).

[9]   OWEN JONES ET AL., LAW AND NEUROSCIENCE 3 (2d ed. 2020).

[10] Miller v. Alabama, 567 U.S. 460, 472 n.5 (2012) (barring mandatory life-without-parole sentence for juvenile offenders in homicide cases); Graham v. Florida, 560 U.S. 48, 68–74 (2010) (barring mandatory life-

without-parole sentence for juvenile offenders in non-homicide cases); Roper v. Simmons, 543 U.S. 551, 569–78 (2005) (barring the death penalty for crimes committed by juvenile offenders).

[11] ADAM COHEN, IMBECILES: THE SUPREME COURT, AMERICAN EUGENICS, AND THE STERILIZATION OF CARRIE BUCK 8–9, 299–300, 319 (2016).

[12] Adina Schwartz, *A Systemic Challenge to the Reliability and Admissibility of Firearms and Toolmark Identification*, 6 COLUM. SCI. & TECH. L. REV. 2, *3 (2005).

[13] Joshua Greene & Jonathan Cohen, *For the Law, Neuroscience Changes Nothing and Everything*, 359 PHIL. TRANSACTIONS ROYAL SOC'Y LONDON 1775, 1775 (2004).

[14] Francis X. Shen, *Neurolegislation: How U.S. Legislators Are Using Brain Science*, 29 HARV. J.L. & TECH. 495, 498 (2016).

[15] James R. P. Ogloff, *Two Steps Forward and One Step Backward: The Law and Psychology Movement(s) in the 20th Century*, 24 L. & HUMAN BEHAV. 457, 477 (2000).

[16] Harry Kalven, Jr., *The Quest for the Middle Range: Empirical Inquiry and Legal Policy*, *in* LAW IN A CHANGING AMERICA 56, 65, 67 (Geoffrey Hazard, Jr. ed. 1968).

[17] Bleistein v. Donaldson Lithographing Co, 188 U.S. 239, 251–52 (1903).

[18] Diego Fernandez-Duque et al., *Superfluous Neuroscience Information Makes Explanations of Psychological Phenomena More Appealing*, 27 J. COGNITIVE NEUROSCI. 926 (2015); David P. McCabe et al., *The Influence of fMRI Lie Detection Evidence on Juror Decision-Making*, 29 BEHAV. SCI. & L. 566 (2011).

PART I

The Law and Neuroscience of Creative Activity

1 COPYRIGHT AND CREATIVITY

Policy decisions in pursuit of creativity shape many if not most of the environments in which we live. Businesses design workplaces to unlock innovative thought. Urban planners set city priorities in an effort to attract "the creative class." Teachers adjust their pedagogy to encourage creative thinking in students. Intellectual property law is no exception. To earn a patent, inventors must exercise more than "ordinary creativity."[1] Creativity receives the greatest amount of legal attention in copyright law, with it being settled doctrine that that area of law's "fundamental objective" is "to foster creativity."[2]

At the same time, the creative process has long represented a mystery – its importance recognized but its secrets closely held. Artists themselves offer little insight, referring to the act of creation as "magic" or "subconscious." Frustrated judges complain of their inability to understand the process or recognize truly creative works for what they are.

Creativity's unknowable nature is beginning to change, however. Inquiries into the biology of creative thought, which now represent a large share of all psychological studies of creativity, bring new insights into the creative process – insights that clash with the uninformed guesses of a century's worth of copyright jurisprudence. What the research shows is that creative activity has certain hallmarks – and that these hallmarks are disregarded in contemporary copyright law. There is plenty of blame to go around for the law's misguided approach to evaluating creativity, but the main malefactor is one of the most renowned judges of all time: Oliver Wendell Holmes.

A "SUBSTANTIVELY IMPOTENT" TEST

There is a creativity paradox at the heart of American copyright law. On the one hand, statements as to the centrality of creativity to copyright protection are omnipresent. According to the US Supreme Court, the "ultimate aim" of copyright law is "to stimulate artistic creativity for the general public good."[3] Hearing this message, lower courts repeatedly describe the promotion of creativity as copyright law's guiding purpose. To this end, the law requires every copyrightable work to be "original," and every work must demonstrate creativity in order to be considered original.[4]

On the other hand, for all its supposed importance, copyright's creativity requirement is a paper tiger. Ill-defined, the requirement remains inchoate, anchored only by words and phrases indicating just how skimpy this requirement is. In announcing a formal creativity requirement in 1991, the Supreme Court used terms like "minimal," "low," "slight," and "modicum."[5] According to another court, "just a scintilla of creativity" will do.[6] Scholars describe the creativity requirement as "substantively impotent," "uncertain and confused," and playing "little or no useful role in copyright analysis."[7]

In fact, courts do their best to avoid any scrutiny of the requirement, hastily determining that the bare minimum of needed imagination exists and then moving on to other legal issues. Rather than putting any teeth into the requirement, judges award copyright protection to works that are entirely conventional as well as ones that are completely accidental. For example, management training materials so bland that they were described as "aggressively vapid," so filled with jargon and "platitudinal business speak" that a judge thought they could be grist for satirical send-ups of workplace culture like the sitcom *The Office* and the film *Office Space*, and so "obvious" that they offered nothing more than "common sense" were still considered sufficiently creative.[8] It is hard to argue that the requirement is furthering copyright law's ultimate goal of spurring artistic creativity when its application in actual cases represents the kind of test that everyone passes.

Courts go to great lengths to avoid denying copyright protection to a work for lack of creativity. Less-than-inspired song lyrics, like repetition of the phrase "uh oh," have been considered sufficiently creative.[9]

Even when elements of a work are identical to another work, judges take pains to downplay glaring similarities that augur against creativity. When pop diva Mariah Carey was accused of infringement, Carey maintained the other artist's song was insufficiently creative to enjoy copyright protection. In support, she noted that a seven-note sequence in the first measure of the song was identical to the first measure of the folk song "For He's a Jolly Good Fellow." A federal court rejected Carey's argument, reasoning that the first measure could be creative in the musical genre of R&B, even if it was uncreative in folk music.[10]

This is not to say that the creativity requirement is a completely empty vessel. There is a certain zone where someone's attempt to create is not creative enough to warrant copyright protection – otherwise the Supreme Court's pronouncement of a creativity requirement would be fatuous. But this zone only occupies the "narrowest and most obvious limits."[11] Most famously, in the case of *Feist Publications* v. *Rural Telephone Service*, the Supreme Court denied copyright protection for a telephone directory listing names, addresses, and phone numbers by alphabetical order. "[T]here is nothing remotely creative about arranging names alphabetically in a white pages directory," the Court explained.[12] Copyright has also been denied for lack of creativity for random number generation,[13] a single sentence posted to a listserv,[14] and a chart listing horse-racing statistics in a functional grid.[15]

Yet such cases are the exceptions that prove the rule. Only in situations where it is difficult to discern any degree of choice or selection in the plaintiff's work is there the possibility for a judgment that creativity is lacking. In *Feist*, the Court deemed the alphabetical ordering of names insufficiently creative because such ordering was "universally observed," "so commonplace that it has come to be expected as a matter of course," and "practically inevitable."[16] Likewise, the terse listserv post asking about an accounting firm's billing practices and the grid listing dates and betting amounts for horse races arguably had few ways to be alternately composed. Copyright was denied for random number generation because it was "arbitrary," i.e., it involved no selection at all.[17]

Creativity surely means more than making a choice between two options. In the popular imagination, creativity refers to acts of extraordinary talent.[18] For their part, courts use phrases like "creative judgment," "intellectual conception," "intellectual invention," "true artistic skill," and "intellectual production" to describe creativity. At the same time, however, they are extremely generous in considering works that are the product of very few intellectual choices as creative. Seemingly uncreative works – from an exact miniature copy of an existing sculpture, to a standardized test answer sheet, to instruction manuals, to the use of arrows and placement of text in a catalog to highlight particular products – are routinely deemed sufficiently creative.[19]

The law's generous approach to creativity has consequences. Without a true screen for artistic originality, just about every communication becomes the subject of copyright protection. In the mid-1970s, Congress abrogated the formalities once required to enjoy a copyrightable interest, like affixing a notice of copyright to the work or registering the work with the government. Copyright protection now automatically springs into being without the need for notice, registration, or other any affirmative action from the author.[20] Congress has also dramatically expanded the length of copyright protection, moving from a mere twenty-eight-year term (with the possibility of renewal for a second twenty-eight years) at the beginning of the twentieth century to a current duration of the life of the author plus seventy years more. The end result is an ever-growing avalanche of copyrighted content. When every social media post and selfie snap, no matter how pedestrian, becomes the subject of a copyright for more than a century, the amount of material available in the public domain for true artistic output shrinks. Meanwhile, the population becomes an unwitting army of infringers as they violate copyright each time they resend or repost someone else's expression. Some fear the growing chasm between the letter of the law and citizen behavior threatens the viability of copyright law itself.[21] Many different legal rules contribute to this law/norm gap, but at least some of the fault lies in decisions pronouncing almost any expressive act sufficiently creative to warrant copyright protection.

Why has copyright law fallen into this paradox? Why not heighten the creativity requirement, as some legal scholars have suggested, so that it is doing work to actually incentivize originality in authors and preserve an expansive public domain? The reasons why this path to resolving the paradox has not been taken have to do with judicial understandings of the nature of creativity itself. As described below, the requirement's anemic state specifically stems from legal choices to blind judges and juries to key information – an author's intentions toward their work and the work's reception in the relevant artistic community – that could be used to raise the creativity bar. The courts consider such information immaterial; neuroscience reveals it is directly relevant to understanding the creative process.

THE ACCIDENTAL AUTHOR

Courts have adopted their minimalist conception of the creativity requirement out of a belief that creativity is impossible to measure. If the creative process is unavoidably subjective – a form of "magic" understandable only to the artist herself and perhaps not even to her – then the courts should avoid paying it much attention. Instead of interrogating a question for which there is no probative evidence, courts should simply presume creativity in all but the rarest of cases.

This view is best represented by Oliver Wendell Holmes's influential majority opinion in the case of *Bleistein* v. *Donaldson Lithographing Co.* The 1903 case, which involved the copyrightability of poster art advertising a traveling circus, sets an extremely low bar for satisfying the originality requirement and adopts a correspondingly generous view of human creativity. As described by Holmes, the creative process is natural, inevitable, and found in everyone: "Personality always contains something unique. It expresses its singularity even in handwriting, and a very modest grade of art has in it something irreducible which is one man's alone."[22]

This description of creative thought as mere "personality" is far different from the one in the popular imagination. Most people consider something creative by virtue of its statistical infrequency. Yet Holmes rejected the popular definition for the courts, at least in part, because creativity is so difficult to evaluate. His description of creativity as inherently personal signaled a belief that creativity is not susceptible to outside measurement. Because artistic works cannot be judged in any objective fashion, copyright law had to impose a subjective standard of originality.

One might assume that this stance would have led courts to examine the artist's own mindset for evidence of creativity. Even if the court's measurement of a work's creativity against some objective scale is improper, consideration of the artist's own subjective beliefs during the creative process might help provide at least some data for a creativity assessment. If someone sets out to be creative, maybe it is more likely that they will succeed in being creative. We see such analyses in other legal regimes. Scrutiny of mental state is a central component of many if not most areas of the law from determining *mens rea* for different crimes to looking for the presence or absence of a particular state of mind in tort law (e.g., actual malice in a defamation case). Indeed, many areas of copyright law, outside of the evaluation of creativity, take pains to scrutinize the motivations of the parties.[23]

Despite all of these other areas of willingness to consider evidence of mental state, copyright doctrine insists that any inquiry into the motivations of an author is improper when evaluating creativity. Objections to such inquiries are longstanding. In 1945, Judge Jerome Frank sounded the alarm against using a would-be author's intentions to determine if his changes to an existing work were sufficient to be considered original. A prominent New Dealer and legal scholar before he became a judge, Frank's innovative decisions exerted a lasting impact on copyright as well as other areas of the law. Like Holmes, Frank's objection to evidence of authorial intent stemmed from concerns over the inability of outsiders to understand the creative process. "It is not easy to ascertain what is intended and what inadvertent in the work of genius," he explained. "That a man is color blind may make him a master of black and white art; a painter's unique distortions, hailed as a sign of his genius, may be due to defective muscles."[24]

Six years later, Frank reaffirmed his position in the case of *Alfred Bell* v. *Catalda Fine Arts*. In that case, the plaintiff asserted copyright in mezzotint engravings of paintings from the late eighteenth and early nineteenth centuries. Mezzotinting involves using a roughened metal plate to make a print of another work. Frank deemed the engraved reproductions copyrightable, explaining that originality "means little more than a prohibition on actual copying." Even though the plaintiff's avowed goal was to reproduce the original paintings as accurately as possible, because the mezzotinting process could not produce perfect replicas, the plaintiff could not be accused of "actual copying." The fact that the subtle changes and imperfections in the mezzotinted works the plaintiff sought to protect were unintentional did not matter to Frank. "[E]ven if their substantial departures from the paintings were inadvertent, the copyrights would be valid," he explained. Frank even speculated that mistakes made when translating a literary work from one language to another would similarly be eligible for copyright protection.[25]

Frank's call to ignore consideration of artist motivations echoes throughout more modern cases. In a case involving promotional photographs taken of copyrighted toys, the holder of copyrights in the toys maintained that because the photographer intended the photos for the "purely utilitarian function" of identifying products for consumers, the photographs were ineligible for copyright protection. The court rejected this argument, explaining that the "purpose of the photographs" was irrelevant to the originality analysis.[26] Another court analyzed the copyrightability of photographs, this time of automobile transmission parts for a catalog. The court held the photographs copyrightable, explaining that it did not matter how the plaintiff thought about its design process or that it embarked on its catalog project with no creative conception in mind.[27] This discounting of the importance of artistic mindset can be found in the frequent incantation in modern copyright decisions that it is the ultimate product that matters for the creativity requirement, not the process that led to that product.[28]

The assumption that creativity is detached from motivation reaches its apotheosis in judicial discussion of works that are the product of accident. If the purpose of copyright protection is to incentivize the production of creative works, there would seem to be no need to grant protection to accidental creations. After all, an author or artist who creates inadvertently cannot be said to have been incentivized by the law. Given that copyright protection imposes costs on downstream actors by blocking them from using someone else's copyrighted materials, a strong argument can be made for excluding accidental creations from the benefits of copyright protection.

Nevertheless, the law is quite clear that accidental works of art not only satisfy the creativity requirement but they receive just as much protection and benefit as works that were the conscious products of artistic genius. In *Alfred Bell*, Frank shared a story from the ancient Greek philospher Plutarch. According to the story, "A painter, enraged because he could not depict the foam that filled a horse's mouth from champing at the bit, threw a sponge at his painting; the sponge splashed against the wall – and achieved the desired result."[29] The implication of the story seems to be that artistic products of accident are just as deserving of copyright as any other work eligible for copyright protection. In accord, courts today routinely mention that copyright protection applies to accidental steps and unconscious choices. As the leading copyright treatise explains, "[t]he independent effort that constitutes originality may be inadvertent and still satisfy the requirements of copyright."[30]

NO SKILLS OR TRAINING NECESSARY

At the same time that the creativity requirement eschews subjective inquiry into authorial motives, it also refuses other means to scrutinize an author's creative capabilities. Evidence of an author's skill or training in the art is not considered when assessing creativity. Contrasting authors with inventors, a late nineteenth-century court explained that the latter term implies the use of more than "only ordinary skill" whereas the former requires little skill as evidenced by the "multitude of books [that] rest safely under copyright." The court listed various lowbrow works found to enjoy copyright, including a dramatic scene of someone being rescued from a speeding train and a comic song called "Slap, Bang, Here We Are Again!" to demonstrate that "the courts have not undertaken … to measure the degree of originality, or literary skill or training involved."[31]

Along similar lines, more modern decisions hold that the amateur status of photographers and videographers is no barrier to passing the creativity threshold.[32] After the Supreme Court in *Feist* instructed that mere "sweat of brow" does not render something creative, lower courts took pains to emphasize that the author's skill in the art did not impact their creativity determinations.[33] Martin Scorsese is no more likely to meet the necessary creativity threshold than anyone with an iPhone.

If expertise makes one no more likely to be creative, it also makes one no more capable of assessing creativity in others. In *Bleistein,* Holmes bolstered the case for a minimalist creativity standard with a closing prudential argument that still shapes the contours of copyright law over a century later. He maintained that even if a court were somehow capable of assessing creativity, the dangers of aesthetic discrimination were not worth the risk:

> It would be a dangerous undertaking for persons trained only to the law to constitute themselves final judges of the worth of pictorial illustrations, outside of the narrowest and most obvious limits. At the one extreme, some works of genius would be sure to miss appreciation. Their very novelty would make them repulsive until the public had learned the new language in which their author spoke. It may be more than doubted, for instance, whether the etchings of Goya or the paintings of Manet would have been sure of protection when seen for the first time. At the other end, copyright would be denied to pictures which appealed to a public less educated than the judge. Yet if they command the interest of any public, they have a commercial value – it would be bold to say that they have not an aesthetic and educational value – and the taste of any public is not to be treated with contempt.[34]

Because the twin mysteries of artistic genius and mass appeal must always remain somewhat opaque to judges, the argument goes, it is better to simply allow all but the most egregious copyists to claim the "creative" mantle.

Holmes was not just singling out judges as somehow failing to recognize innovative art at the time it is made. Throughout the opinion, he dropped references to various European artistic masters, revealing his own erudition as well as the limits of his supposedly self-deprecatory stance. Holmes knew that he, and many other judges, actually knew quite a lot about art. His position was that *no one* could appreciate artistic contributions in their own time, necessarily implicating art world experts as well as judges and everyone else. By articulating a view of experts as always behind the creativity curve, Holmes walled off informed outsiders from offering help to judges trying to decide whether something was creative or not.

A century later, Holmes is applauded for banishing credentialism and expert gatekeepers from the creativity determination and thereby making admission to the society of copyright holders "democratic."[35] The modern creativity requirement displays the same judicial antipathy to aesthetic expertise as courts decline to rely on expert testimony to certify originality. Judges invoke various strategies to exclude or discount such testimony. One tactic is to reprimand the expert for applying too high of a creativity standard in order to ignore their testimony. Judges also reject expert testimony on creativity for usurping the role of the trier of fact. As one court explained in justifying its exclusion of experts on both sides of a case involving jewelry designs, expert testimony on "the subjects of originality and creativity ... [is] analogous to having expert witnesses testify in a personal injury action that a party's conduct was negligent," an issue exclusively within the province of the judge or jury.[36]

So if the courts cannot look to authorial skill or expert opinion to assess creativity, what can they use? The substitute for undemocratically taking into account individual authorial capabilities or trained judgment in the creativity analysis is to rely solely on market forces. If someone had the financial motive to replicate your work, that is proof that your work is creative. The leading treatise on copyright maintains that if someone copies off you, it must mean that what you did was creative: "[O]ne may initially posit that, if any author's independent efforts contain sufficient skill to motivate another's copying, there is ipso facto a sufficient quantum of originality to support a copyright."[37] Along the same lines, the *Bleistein* decision instructs that originality of a combination of expressive elements "is sufficiently shown by the desire to reproduce them without regard to plaintiff's rights."[38] More modern courts adopt the same logic. For example, the label on Pledge furniture polish was deemed copyrightable because a rival polish manufacturer intentionally used a similar label.[39]

Although there is a bit of circular reasoning in using the presence of copying to satisfy copyright's creativity requirement, we can see how this approach is in keeping with a democratic view of artists and artistry. Copyright's current creativity test does not pick winners and losers. By judging creativity only through the economic incentives of others to copy, courts can avoid charges of aesthetic elitism. Equating creativity with mere personality enacts an egalitarian vision of the creative process that respects everyone's creative potential, but at the cost of considering almost everyone and anything they produce legally creative. Behind these doctrinal choices is a view of creativity as inherently unknowable to outside parties. As we will see, even if it was once true that creativity is impervious to outside measurement, this state of affairs has changed thanks to the techniques and tools of neuroscience.

CREATIVITY: A NEUROSCIENTIFIC VIEW

Psychologists have been attempting to unlock the secrets of the creative process for decades. Much of their early efforts polled artists themselves, but with little yield. Artists refer to a process that is indescribable, confirming the instinct of legal actors that artistic creativity is impossible to measure. A typical example comes from the experimental composer Leo Ornstein. "I have no theory," he said. "I don't write music out of any preconceived theory at all. I just write what I hear. Sometimes as a matter of fact ... some of the things I have written ... I wonder why I should have heard what I did. I can't explain it to myself."[40] Or take this pronouncement from Bruce Springsteen: "Creativity is an act of magic rising up from your subconscious."[41] Unable to learn from artists' own recountings, some psychologists resorted to Freudian theory, attributing creative behavior to the sublimation of sexual desires, a view of creativity that has now been discredited.[42]

Yet if talking to and psychoanalyzing artists was a mostly losing proposition, using neuroscience to study the creative process has generated significant insights. Instead of relying on self-reporting, neuroscientists examine the neural activity of artists as they are engaged in creative tasks such as generating a humorous caption for a cartoon, improvising music, or crafting a metaphor to capture the meaning of a given adjective. For these experiments, experts in the relevant artistic domain independently evaluate each artistic output for its relative creativity compared to the group of outputs as a whole. If the expert rankings display a sufficient level of consensus, their creativity ratings are considered valid. The outputs can then be ranked on a spectrum of low to high creativity and compared against each participant's neural behavior. To those who question how any study can proclaim itself able to separate the creative wheat from the non-creative chaff, it has been shown time and time again that the use of expert panels offers high intra-panel reliability. Regardless of the domain studied, experts in a domain tend to agree in their judgment of expressive works. The same is not true when researchers ask novices to rate artistic output for its creativity.[43]

Perhaps the chief revelation from this research has been an ability to measure what was once unmeasurable. Contrary to the central premise of *Bleistein* and a century of copyright creativity jurisprudence, some aspects of the creative process can be objectively quantified. Not every part of the creative process can be tracked and mapped by neuroscientists. But even a partial inventory of this process represents a great leap forward in understanding. A brief description of research on "alpha waves," the physiology of mental imagery, and the connectivity of relevant brain regions illustrates the objective means neuroscientists can offer for describing creative success and failure.

Findings involving alpha waves represent some of "the most consistent findings" in creativity neuroscience.[44] EEG (electroencephalogram) signals oscillate over a variety of frequencies. These frequencies are divided into a series of frequency bands. It is possible to compute the band-specific frequency power for different periods of time and to contrast the power in a specific frequency during a cognitive task and compare this reading to a referent when the task is not being performed.

Studies consistently reveal increased activity in the "alpha" EEG frequency band during particular aspects of creative thinking. For example, college students rated "highly creative" by their instructors exhibited higher alpha signals during the inspiration phase (as opposed to the elaboration phase) of a creative writing project but no such difference existed for the less creative students.[45] More recent research allows for a more fine-grained view of creative ideation by dividing the broad alpha range into several sub-frequencies. Lower frequencies in this range are more likely to apply to general task demands like alertness and attention whereas higher frequencies are more sensitive to specific task requirements like recalling relevant words or numbers from memory. Other studies show relationships between types of alpha activation and a person's subjective rating of their own ideas as original as well as more successful performance of different creative activities, including, for example, improvisational dance.[46] These findings do not tell nearly all of the story when it comes to creative thought. But the "reliable and robust" relationship between alpha power and creative ideation shows that objective measurement of some aspects of creative thought is entirely possible.[47]

Neuroscience also allows us to distinguish between creative and non-creative uses of internal images. Intuitively, we already associate the creative process with the generation of mental imagery. It turns out that the generation of such imagery is critical to visual and non-visual creativity alike. Not all uses of imagery are creative. For example, merely recollecting previously seen images is not a sign of creative activity. Having a photographic memory might be useful in life, but it does not make someone an artist. Luckily, scientists can distinguish between the neural correlates of new mental images and the signs of retrieving old images from memory. They conclude that the brain's imagining of new images "certainly represents a crucial capacity underlying creative thought."[48]

Finally, neuroscience tells us that the stronger the interplay between three particular brain systems, the more creative the person. When the strength of a person's connections in this neural network is measured, that measurement strongly correlates with how someone performs on a test for originality. Researchers find "a person's capacity to generate original ideas can be reliably predicted from the strength of functional connectivity within this network, indicating that creative thinking ability is characterized by a distinct brain connectivity profile."[49] For example, the greater the coupling between the brain's default and executive control networks, the better test subjects completed an exercise asking them to suggest uncommon verbs to pair with a given noun.[50]

Nothing I have written thus far should imply that neuroscience can precisely measure creativity or that current technologies can provide admissible neurological evidence of a particular creator's mental state. Creativity is a complicated mental process that scientists continue to explore. Some parts of creative ideation have moved into sharper focus thanks to neuroscience. Others, like the incubation period needed for some creative insights, are less susceptible to testing in a laboratory setting. Adding to the difficulty, the brain regions studied in these tests of creativity can be involved in many different activities, not just creative expression.

Nevertheless, two decades of creativity neuroscience studies provide some valuable lessons. Some stages of the creative process are more amenable to neural study than others, but even a partial understanding of this process is better than none. Reverse inference is a concern, but if applied carefully, it can have significant predictive power and reveal useful correlations that can be further tested. Most importantly, neuroscientific study of the creative process is uncovering evidence of mental phenomena that we are not aware of or cannot describe ourselves. Because we lack the tools to articulate the creative process as it occurs in our heads, neuroscientific research offers a particularly promising mechanism for understanding this process. Measurements of alpha waves, mental imagery, and inter-network connectivity do not tell us everything we need to know about creativity but they do offer objective details of a behavior that *Bleistein* and other copyright decisions assumed had to remain shrouded in mystery. More specifically, this research reveals that the evidentiary items deemed irrelevant by the courts – artistic motivation and expertise – are not just relevant but are essential elements in understanding human creativity.

MOTIVATION

There is widespread agreement among psychologists studying creativity that motivation is a vital element of creative activity. Motivation increases artistic skill. Intentional seeking of novelty is critical to creative success. The neuroscientist Antonio Damasio puts motivation at the top of his list for requirements for human creativity.[51]

To the extent copyright law is meant to promote creativity, it would seem that it should reward motivated creative behavior and not reward non-creative behavior or behavior that accidentally produces novel artistic output. Psychologists note that motivation results in more creative ideas being generated. Someone who is unmotivated may generate only one solution to the task at hand whereas a motivated artist is likely to generate many, resulting in greater and superior creative production. In other words, motivated artists are more productive and the more productive you are, the greater the chance that you will hit upon some creative ideas in your different artistic outputs. The accidental creation of art described by Plutarch – a painter throws a sponge in anger and inadvertently creates a masterpiece – is not the way the vast majority of artistic breakthroughs are made. "[M]ore often than not, the unconventional tendencies of truly creative people are intentional and discretionary. They know what they are doing."[52]

Two particular attributes relating to motivation strongly correlate with creative output. Focus, which can be detected by the techniques of neuroscience, is a key ingredient in artistic production. Creativity demands an ability to ignore outside stimuli. According to creativity researchers, originality requires the capability "to stay deeply absorbed in self-generated thoughts, despite the constant exposition of potentially interfering sensory stimulation."[53] A variety of studies links focused attention to success on divergent thinking tasks, i.e., tasks that involve coming up with multiple solutions to a problem, a favorite metric for evaluating creative potential.[54] Neural scans describe a relationship between focused attention and success in generating novel ideas.[55]

The focus necessary for creative activity is not just to keep out external stimuli. Artists also need to be single-minded enough to inhibit their own habitual responses. This may be why high originality scores on a variety of creative projects correlate with brain areas that relate to executive actions. Innovators need to be able to block out the voices in their heads that tell them to take the cognitive path of least resistance by doing things in a routine or traditional way or by simply copying what came before. Originality demands that we ignore internal and external forces that draw us to the average and the familiar.

Artists must not only be able to focus on the task at hand, but commit themselves to sustained action in pursuit of a creative goal. Most psychologists believe that the creative process occurs in various phases and that the process begins with an early "preparation" phase that is "difficult and time-consuming," rather than sudden and effortless.[56] "[C]reativity isn't a burst of inspiration; it's mostly conscious hard work."[57] Studies of successful creators show this to be the case. For example, artists spend more time reworking their drawings than non-artists.[58]

Copyright law has long been enamored of metaphors suggesting that artistic creativity appears like a bolt of lightning out of nowhere as with the story of Plutarch's painter. The *Feist* decision amplified this unfortunate tendency to equate creativity with speed. In that case, the Court used the phrase "creative spark" to describe what was needed to satisfy the creativity requirement, suggesting that artistic creativity is a sudden and unforeseeable phenomenon. Along similar lines, the *Alfred Bell* decision attributed copyrightable material to the immediate influence on the artist of a "clap of thunder."[59]

Metaphors involving sparks and claps of thunder oversimplify the creative process and promote the false narrative of the accidental artist. Creativity involves multiple stages that take a significant amount of time. By portraying creativity as a sudden phenomenon that comes out of nowhere, copyright law's operative metaphors imply that focus and sustained effort are irrelevant to the creative process. In truth, "[c]-reative thought involves the generation of complex mental representations that need to be maintained over extended periods of time for stimulation and elaboration."[60]

This is not to say that creative problem-solving occurs in a linear, even-paced fashion. There are moments of insight. EEG studies are particularly suited to uncovering particular brain regions involved in those moments, which can involve seemingly sudden shifts in perspective. But it is important to realize that these moments of insight are not all that is needed to generate something that is new and appropriate to the artistic undertaking. It turns out that creative activity requires control over both outside stimuli that threaten to break our concentration and internal forces that threaten to distract us from the task at hand. Creativity is rarely speedy and rarely an accident. "Even when ideas come in a flash, focus and persistence are required to put them to good use."[61]

EXPERTISE

Copyright law's anti-expert posture enacts two myths about the creative process into the substance of copyright law. First, the law presumes that we are equally situated for creative success, ignoring evidence of authorial experience and training. In truth, our creative abilities differ. This is probably no surprise to most of us. We have our own thoughts about how creative we are compared to the average person. Recent neuroscientific studies provide a wealth of evidence confirming the unequal distribution of creative capacity. Most important for our purposes, these studies reveal that the likelihood of generating creative output is strongly correlated with expertise.

Sheer familiarity with an art form produces dramatic physiological differences during creative thought. In one experiment, neuroscientists scanned the brains of experienced professional comedians, aspiring comedians, and a control group possessing the same high intelligence as the rest of the research subjects but with no experience as comedians. All were given the task of coming up with captions for a blank *New Yorker* cartoon. Although it might seem that the quality of humorous creations is subjective, it turns out that humor typically has high agreement across individuals and can be evaluated for quality through rankings as well as by listening for spontaneous laughter in audiences. The study revealed significant differences in the experts' brain functioning while they devised their captions as compared to the other participants.[62]

Other research reveals differences in neural responses based on experience. Experienced writers show stronger activation of the brain regions associated with memory retrieval and emotion processing than inexperienced writers.[63] Familiarity with professional design concepts facilitates the inhibition of irrelevant visual memories in the brain's prefrontal cortex, allowing greater focus on the development of a new industrial design.[64] This biological data complements older research claiming that those recognized for great creative achievements needed significant amounts of time to master their discipline. A common postulate in the literature is that theoretical breakthroughs typically require ten years of deep involvement in a domain.

It is not just experience but the kind of experience someone has in an artistic discipline that matters. "Brain imaging studies have found that people with musical training actually think about music differently, people with artistic training actually think about art differently, and people with dance training think about dance differently."[65] Contrary to the popular belief that lengthy periods of institutional schooling stunt creative potential, there is no slump in creativity as training continues. Children are no more likely to be creative than adults. Given this research, scientists now believe that even spontaneous creative mental states are better fostered through systematic institutional training than informal training or no training at all.[66]

The second myth contends that no one – not even experts – can appreciate the aesthetic avant-garde. This was one of Justice Holmes's prudential arguments for broadening the definition of artistic creativity to include anything that is the "personal reaction of an individual upon nature." Holmes warned that if courts failed to take such a hands-off approach to copyright's creativity requirement, new "works of genius" from modern-day Manets would be cast aside since they could not be aesthetically appreciated in their own times.

Creativity research calls Holmes's supposition into doubt, at least when it comes to experts in the relevant domain. One enduring misconception about creativity in Western societies is that creative people are so far ahead of the rest of us that their brilliance can never be appreciated during their lifetime. Creativity scholar R. Keith Sawyer contends that, in actuality, most creative contributions are fully recognized as such at the time they are made.[67] Many of the most important creative contributions result not from something that transforms the discipline but from a relatively straightforward process like redefinition or combination of two previously uncombined fields. These are creative leaps whose value can be appreciated by experts when they occur. Quantitative studies confirm that artistic reputations stay consistent over time and it is rare for a previously unrecognized artist to be embraced as a genius after death.[68]

Holmes also raised the specter of judges privileging what they know rather than what is new when it comes to expressive works. This concern could surely apply to experts as well. Bias toward the familiar is certainly a risk when evaluating new forms of expression. But familiarity bias is a risk when evaluating all sorts of things, not just art. Despite Holmes' concerns, the creativity requirement need not be synonymous with judicial taste for the familiar. Instead, it is possible to evaluate creative contributions against a baseline of what has come before rather than by an expert's or a judge's personal preference. Judges already perform this sort of analysis when ensuring that inventive activity must be "nonobvious" to be eligible for patent protection. Along similar lines, a more specified creativity standard could prompt judges to look for art that represents some departure from the status quo.

Truly creative works are not happy accidents. Neuroscience confirms that they are the product of a particular process that involves lengthy planning, deliberation, and focus. Yet judges blind themselves to information on the creative *process*, evaluating creativity by exclusive reference to the final *product* – the allegedly creative work itself – and repeatedly insisting that even accidental and unconscious conduct can be creative. Considering authorial motivation and expertise in the relevant artistic domain could bolster the creativity requirement and bring copyright law into better alignment with the means by which creative works are actually born.

Notes

1 Intercontinental Great Brands, LLC v. Kellogg N. Am. Co., 869 F.3d 1336, 1346 (Fed. Cir. 2017).
2 Warner Bros. v. ABC, 720 F.2d 231, 240 (2d Cir. 1983).
3 Twentieth Century Music Corp. v. Aiken, 422 U.S. 151, 156 (1975).
4 Feist Publ'ns v. Rural Tele. Serv. Co., 499 U.S. 340, 345–46 (1991).
5 *Id.* at 345–46, 362.
6 Luck's Music Library, Inc. v. Ashcroft, 321 F. Supp. 2d 107, 118 (D.D.C. 2004).
7 Dennis S. Karjala, *Copyright and Creativity*, 15 UCLA ENT. L. REV. 169, 171 (2008); Michael J. Madison, *Beyond Creativity: Copyright as Knowledge Law*, 12 VAND. J. ENT. & TECH. L. 817, 830 (2010); Dale P. Olson, *Copyright Originality*, 48 Mo. L. REV. 29, 31 (1983).
8 Situation Mgmt. Sys. v. ASP Consulting Grp., 560 F.3d 53, 60 (1st Cir. 2009).
9 Santrayll v. Burrell, 39 U.S.P.Q.2d 1052 (S.D.N.Y. 1996). See also Tin Pan Apple, Inc. v. Miller Brewing Co., 30 U.S.P.Q.2d 1791 (S.D.N.Y. 1994) (rap song lyrics "Hugga-Hugga" and "Brr" sufficiently creative).
10 Swirsky v. Carey, 376 F.3d 841, 850 (9th Cir. 2004).

[11] ABS Entm't, Inc. v. CBS Corp., 908 F.3d 405, 422 (9th Cir. 2018).

[12] Feist, 499 U.S. at 363.

[13] Mitel, Inc. v. Iqtel, Inc., 124 F.3d 1355, 1374 (10th Cir. 1997).

[14] Stern v. Does, 978 F. Supp. 2d 1031, 1042 (C.D. Cal. 2011).

[15] Victor Lalli Enters., Inc. v. Big Red Apple, Inc., 936 F.2d 671, 673 (2d Cir. 1991).

[16] Feist, 499 U.S. at 363.

[17] Mitel, 124 F.3d at 1373–74.

[18] Phillip McIntyre, *Creativity and Cultural Production: A Study of Contemporary Popular Western Music Songwriting*, 20 CREATIVITY RES. J. 20, 20 (2008). Psychologists largely agree on a definition of creativity as requiring something that is new and appropriate to the circumstances. Dean Keith Simonton, *Taking the U.S. Patent Office Criteria Seriously: A Quantitative Three-Criterion Creativity Definition and Its Implications*, 24 CREATIVITY RES. J. 97, 97 (2012).

[19] Eagle Servs. Corp. v. H2O Indus. Servs., 532 F.3d 620, 622–23 (7th Cir. 2008); Decker Inc. v. G & N Equip. Co., 438 F. Supp. 2d 734, 743 (E.D. Mich. 2006); Harcourt, Brace & World, Inc. v. Graphic Controls Corp., 329 F. Supp. 517, 523–24 (S.D.N.Y. 1971); Alva Studios, Inc. v. Winninger, 177 F. Supp. 265, 267 (S.D.N.Y. 1959).

[20] Though registration is not required for copyright protection, it is required to initiate an action for infringement. 17 § U.S.C. § 411.

[21] JOHN TEHRANIAN, INFRINGEMENT NATION (2011).

[22] 188 U.S. 239, 250 (1903).

[23] See, for example, NXIVM Corp. v. Ross Inst., 364 F.3d 471, 478 (2d Cir. 2004) (bad faith relevant to fair use determination); Past Pluto Prods. Corp. v. Dana, 627 F. Supp. 1435, 1444 (S.D.N.Y. 1986) (intent to avoid infringement considered strong evidence that two works are not substantially similar).

[24] Chamberlin v. Uris Sales Corp., 150 F.2d 512, 513 n.4 (2d Cir. 1945).

[25] Alfred Bell & Co. v. Catalda Fine Arts, 191 F.2d 99, 103, 105–06 (2d Cir. 1951).

[26] Schrock v. Learning Curve Int'l, Inc., 586 F.3d 513 (7th Cir. 2009). See also FrangranceNet.com, Inc. v. FragranceX.com, Inc., 679 F. Supp. 2d 312, 324 n.4 (E.D.N.Y. 2010) (noting that commercial motivation for creation of images "has no bearing on their copyrightability").

[27] Whatever It Takes Transmission & Parts, Inc. v. Capital Core, Inc., No. 2:10-CV-72, 2013 WL 12178585, at *7 (S.D. Ohio Mar. 22, 2013).

[28] ABS Entm't, Inc. v. CBS Corp., 908 F.3d 405, 419 (9th Cir. 2018) ("The process used to create the derivative work is seldom informative of originality in the copyright sense."); Meshwerks, Inc. v. Toyota Motor Sales U.S.A., Inc., 528 F.3d 1258, 1268 (10th Cir. 2008) ("[I]n assessing the originality of

a work for which copyright protection is sought, we look only at the final *product*, not the process.").

29 Alfred Bell & Co. v. Catalda Fine Arts, 191 F.2d 99, 106 n.23 (2d Cir. 1951).

30 1 David Nimmer, Nimmer on Copyright § 2.01 (2020).

31 Henderson v. Tompkins, 60 F. 758, 764 (C.C.D. Mass. 1894).

32 Cruz v. Cox Media Grp., 444 F. Supp. 3d 457, 462, 465 (E.D.N.Y. 2020); Time, Inc. v. Bernard Geis Assocs., 293 F. Supp. 130, 142–43 (S.D.N.Y. 1968).

33 *E.g.*, ABS Entm't, 908 F.3d at 419 ("The remastering engineer's application of intensive, skillful, and even creative labor ... does not guarantee its copyrightability."); Alcatel USA, Inc. v. DGI Techs., Inc., 166 F.3d 772, 789 (5th Cir. 1999) ("[N]o amount of time, labor, skill, and money can bestow copyright eligibility on a work that is devoid of creativity.").

34 Bleistein v. Donaldson Lithographing Co., 188 U.S. 239, 251–52 (1903).

35 Annemarie Bridy, *Coding Creativity: Copyright and the Artificially Intelligent Author*, 2012 Stan. Tech. L. Rev. 5, 6 (describing *Bleistein* as a "democratizing recalibration"); Justin Hughes, *The Photographer's Copyright-Photograph as Art, Photograph as Database*, 25 Harv. J. L. & Tech. 339, 369 (2012) ("*Bleistein* provided American law with an originality threshold low enough that all can enter, giving us a deeply egalitarian, democratic copyright law that has neither place nor need for the creative genius."); Lloyd L. Weinreb, *Copyright for Functional Expression*, 111 Harv. L. Rev. 1149, 1241 (1998) (*Bleistein*'s "[e]schewing any criterion of value except what people are prepared to pay ... has the appeal of the democratic.").

36 Paul Morelli Design, Inc. v. Tiffany & Co., 200 F. Supp. 2d 482, 487 (E.D. Pa. 2002).

37 1 Nimmer, *supra*, at § 2.01.

38 Bleistein, 188 U.S. at 252.

39 Drop Dead Co. v. S. C. Johnson & Son, Inc., 326 F.2d 87, 93 (9th Cir. 1963).

40 Leo Ornstein, Quintette for Piano and Strings, Op. 92, at xxv (2005).

41 David Brooks, *Bruce Springsteen and the Art of Aging Well*, The Atlantic, Oct. 23, 2020.

42 R. Keith Sawyer, Explaining Creativity: The Science of Human Innovation 15–23 (2d ed. 2012).

43 James C. Kaufman et al., *Furious Activity v. Understanding: How Much Expertise Is Needed to Evaluate Creative Work?* 7 Psych. Aesthetics, Creativity & Arts 332, 333 (2013). Quantitative methods can also be used to measure creativity as with divergent thinking tests that are scored based on number on responses as well as the statistical rarity of those responses.

Sameh Said-Metwaly et al., *Approaches to Measuring Creativity: A Systematic Literature Review*, 4 CREATIVITY 238, 245 (2017).

[44] Simone M. Ritter et al., *Eye-Closure Enhances Creative Performance on Divergent and Convergent Creativity Tasks*, 9 FRONTIERS PSYCH. 315, 316 (2018).

[45] Andreas Fink & Mathias Benedek, *EEG Alpha Power and Creative Ideation*, 44 NEUROSCI. & BEHAV. REV. 111, 113 (2014).

[46] Andreas Fink et al., *Brain Correlates Underlying Creative Thinking: EEG Alpha Activity in Professional vs. Novice Dancers*, 46 NEUROIMAGE 854 (2009); Roland H. Grabner et al., *Brain Correlates of Self-Rated Originality of Ideas: Evidence from Event Related Power and Phase-Locking Changes in the EEG*, 121 BEHAV. NEUROSCI. 224 (2007).

[47] Fink & Benedek, *supra*, at 119.

[48] Rex E. Jung et al., *A New Measure of Imagination Ability: Anatomical Brain Imaging Correlates*, 7 FRONTIERS PSYCH. 496 (2016).

[49] Roger E. Beaty et al., *Robust Prediction of Individual Creative Ability from Brain Functional Connectivity*, 115 PROC. NAT'L ACAD. SCI. 1087, 1087 (2018).

[50] Roger E. Beaty et al., *Creative Constraints: Brain Activity and Network Dynamics Underlying Semantic Interference During Idea Production*, 148 NEUROIMAGE 189, 195 (2017).

[51] Antonio R. Damasio, *Some Notes on the Brain, Imagination, and Creativity, in* THE ORIGINS OF CREATIVITY 59, 64–65 (Karl H. Pfenninger & Valerie R. Shubik eds., 2001). See also Panagiotis G. Kampylis & Juri Valtanen, *Redefining Creativity: Analyzing Definitions, Collocations, and Consequences*, 44 J. CREATIVE BEHAV. 191, 198 (2010).

[52] MARK A. RUNCO, CREATIVITY: THEORIES AND THEMES 84 (2007).

[53] Mathias Benedek, *Internally Directed Attention in Creative Cognition, in* CAMBRIDGE HANDBOOK OF THE NEUROSCIENCE OF CREATIVITY 180, 189 (Rex E. Jung & Oshin Vartanian eds. 2018).

[54] Darya L. Zabelina, *Attention and Creativity, in* CAMBRIDGE HANDBOOK OF THE NEUROSCIENCE OF CREATIVITY 161, 164 (Rex E. Jung & Oshin Vartanian eds. 2018).

[55] Mathias Benedek et al., *To Create or to Recall Original Ideas: Brain Processes Associated with the Imagination of Novel Object Uses*, 99 CORTEX 93 (2018).

[56] Ulrich Kraft, *Unleashing Creativity*, 16 SCIENTIFIC AMERICAN MIND 16, 22 (2005).

[57] SAWYER, *supra*, at 387.

[58] Zabelina, *supra*, at 164.

[59] Alfred Bell & Co. v. Catalda Fine Arts, 191 F.2d 99, 105 (2d Cir. 1951).

[60] Benedek, *supra*, at 189.

[61] Zabelina, *supra*, at 164.

[62] Ori Amir & Irving Biederman, *The Neural Correlates of Humor Creativity*, 10 FRONTIERS HUM. NEUROSCI. 1, 1–2, 10 (2016).

[63] Katharina Erhard et al., *Professional Training in Creative Writing Is Associated with Enhanced Fronto-Striatal Activity in a Literary Text Continuation Task*, 100 NEUROIMAGE 15 (2014).

[64] Yasuyuki Kowatari et al., *Neural Networks Involved in Artistic Creativity*, 30 HUM. BRAIN MAPPING 1678 (2009).

[65] SAWYER, *supra*, at 203.

[66] Joel A. Lopata et al., *Creativity as a Distinctly Trainable Mental State: An EEG Study of Musical Improvisation*, 99 NEUROPSYCHOLOGIA 246, 255 (2017).

[67] R. Keith Sawyer, *The Western Cultural Model of Creativity: Its Influence on Intellectual Property Law*, 86 NOTRE DAME L. REV. 2027, 2043 (2011).

[68] DEAN KEITH SIMONTON, GENIUS, CREATIVITY, AND LEADERSHIP 19 (1984); Kathryn Graddy, *Taste Endures! The Rankings of Roger de Piles and Three Centuries of Art Prices*, 73 J. ECON. HIST. 766, 766 (2013).

2   INSIDE THE DESIGN PROCESS

It is not just copyright law that regulates artistic creations; patent law does too. This might come as a surprise to most people. We tend to think of patent law as addressing only the way an article functions, like a machine for separating cotton fibers from their seeds or a method for delivering intravenous fluids to dehydrated patients. But that describes the operation of *utility* patents. *Design* patents are another, less widely known part of the patent system, and they protect the way an article looks rather than the way it works. The original Coca-Cola bottle was the subject of a design patent (pictured in Figure 2.1).[1] So was the Statue of Liberty – the patent allowed the statue's sculptor to control the sale of miniature versions of the statue to raise money for the construction of the full-size version in New York Harbor.[2]

As with copyright, design patent law covers a broad spectrum of creative output, from sculptures to snack trays to computer screen layouts. Design patents have some disadvantages as compared to other forms of intellectual property. Unlike copyright protection, design patent protection lasts for a relatively short time: fifteen years. Also different from copyright and trademark protection, a design patent's focus is exclusively visual – there is no such thing as a design patent in a musical composition or the text of a literary work. Instead of springing into being on their own, a patent (design or utility) must issue from a government agency – the US Patent and Trademark Office (PTO) – a process that takes time and money. Design patents do possess one great advantage over other forms of intellectual property protection, however, in that there is no leeway for unauthorized uses that might be considered non-confusing or "fair use." If someone copies the appearance of your patented design, they are liable for patent infringement – period.

DESIGN.

A. SAMUELSON.
BOTTLE OR SIMILAR ARTICLE.
APPLICATION FILED AUG. 18, 1915

48,160.   Patented Nov. 16, 1915.

FIG. 1.

Figure 2.1 Bottle or similar article, US Patent No. D48,160 (Nov. 16, 1915). The design won a national competition sponsored by the Coca-Cola Company to create a new bottle shape for its product.

Design patents have become a key weapon in the legal arsenal of commercial manufacturers. Two federal court decisions, one announcing a doctrinal change making design patent infringement easier to prove and another ratifying a half a billion dollar verdict for Apple Computer, suddenly catapulted design patent law into a starring role.[3] As a consequence, the number of design patent cases filed in the federal courts climbed exponentially.

It turns out that design patent law was not ready for its close-up. A patentable design must be "nonobvious," which means a design is not protected if "one of ordinary skill would have combined the teachings of the prior art to create the same overall visual appearance as the claimed design."[4] Although this nonobviousness test naturally invites investigations into the thought processes of designers and comparisons to existing designs, courts have declined the invitation. In fact, despite the letter of the law and its rigorous application in the utility patent context, courts largely fail to police design patent applications for nonobviousness, only denying protection when confronted with a single virtually identical prior design. This makes design patents laughably easy to obtain. The reason for this judicial lassitude is a belief that scientific innovation can be detected via objective comparison to past inventive activity whereas innovation in the visual arts does not allow for such a comparison. Neuroscience reveals that this art/science double standard is patently false. Instead, every creative endeavor – whether in the sciences or the visual arts – can only be understood with reference to the prior works and shared assumptions of the relevant domain.

NONOBVIOUSNESS AND ITS RELATIONSHIP TO DESIGN PATENT ELIGIBILITY

To understand the current operation of design nonobviousness, it helps to know a bit about the general requirements for design patent protection. There are three essential criteria for a patentable design. According to federal statute, a protectable design must be "ornamental" and "new." The third requirement, nonobviousness, is judge-made, added through common law decision-making, though subsequently enshrined through legislation.

To be ornamental, the design at issue must not be functional. For example, if a particular shape renders one car mirror more aero-dynamic than all other car mirrors, that shape lacks the necessary ornamentality to be protectable. To avoid the establishment of anti-competitive monopolies around features that make products operate better, functional design elements are supposed to be channeled into the differently calibrated system of utility patents and, therefore, excluded from design patent protection. Design patents are meant to protect things that look good, not things that work well.

The requirement that a design be "new" is referred to as the novelty requirement. Although novelty is determined by the same general rules that apply in the utility patent context – a claimed item fails to satisfy the requirement if the item already exists in the prior art – design patent novelty is comparatively easy to satisfy. Proof of insufficient novelty demands a strict identity between the prior art and the claimed design at issue. Moreover, only ornamental elements can be part of this matching process; any correspondence between the prior art and functional elements in the claimed design is irrelevant. As a consequence, like ornamentality, lack of novelty rarely prevents the issuance of a design patent.

The third, and most important, requirement for design patent eligibility is nonobviousness. A design patent must not issue when "differences between the subject matter sought to be patented and the prior art are such that the subject matter as a whole would have been obvious at the time the invention was made."[5] Though they sound somewhat similar, novelty and nonobviousness are distinct requirements governed by different legal analyses.

Nonobviousness, unlike novelty and ornamentality, is determined from a particular perspective – that of a skilled designer. Nonobviousness is also broader than novelty. For novelty purposes, a successful match requires prior art on all fours with the claimed design. But prior designs, even if not an exact match for the proffered design, can theoretically make the proffered design obvious and therefore invalid. In addition, the nonobviousness assessment can take into account more information than the more restricted novelty determination, which looks only to prior art. For example, the skill of the "ordinary designer" and functional considerations that "teach away" from the claimed design can be considered to assess nonobviousness.

NONOBVIOUSNESS BECOMES A NONISSUE

In the utility patent context, nonobviousness is celebrated as the chief condition for patent protection and one directly linked to patent law's central purpose. It has been referred to as "the heart of the patent system and the justification of patent grants."[6] By limiting patent rights to only those creations that display ingenuity beyond that of the ordinary inventor in the field and truly add to the corpus of human knowledge, the nonobviousness requirement directly aligns with the constitutional edict that patent grants "promote the Progress of Science and useful Arts."[7] As a result, it is generally understood that nonobviousness "stands as the cornerstone of the patent bargain," outshining other patent requirements in importance and theoretical depth.[8]

Despite this celebration in the utility patent context, various decisions by the Federal Circuit – the federal court of appeals responsible for setting out binding interpretations of patent law – have turned design patent nonobviousness into a dead letter. Thanks to two particular doctrinal moves, nonobviousness challenges to a claimed design rarely succeed, either before the PTO or the federal courts. The subtext for these moves is a belief that creativity in the sciences is so different from that in the arts that they must be analyzed in two completely separate ways.

According to the Federal Circuit, every design is nonobvious to a designer unless a single design already exists that is nearly identical to the claimed design. This is far different from nonobviousness in the utility patent context, where various examples of prior art can be combined to reveal that a claimed invention would have been unsurprising to those skilled in the domain. The Federal Circuit also posits that designers adopt a holistic approach to their craft that treats all visual elements of a design equally, none more important than another. Again, this is not at all like the approach to utility patent nonobviousness, where judges are free to focus on those particular components that are most material to the invention. The effect of these moves is to pay little attention to prior designs in judging whether a claimed design warrants patent protection, thereby rendering the nonobviousness requirement a virtual nonentity.

Primary References

Thanks to the Federal Circuit, a finding of obviousness demands two separate inquiries:

> (1) assessing whether a single example from the prior art (called a "primary reference") "creates basically the same visual impression" as the claimed design and (2) determining if that single example, after it has been modified by relevant secondary references, "create[s] a design that has the same overall visual appearance as the claimed design."[9]

Any secondary references must be "so related to the primary reference that the appearance of certain ornamental features in one would suggest the application of those features to the other."[10] If no suitable primary reference exists, there is no need to proceed to the second inquiry and the claimed design cannot be obvious. The determination of suitable primary and secondary references is made from the perspective of a designer with "ordinary skill in the art."[11]

Therefore, to declare a claimed design obvious, there must be a primary reference already in existence having design characteristics that are "basically the same as the claimed design."[12] This exacting standard makes obviousness extremely difficult to prove. For example, in *Apple, Inc.* v. *Samsung Electronics Co.*, the Federal Circuit held that the look of other tablet computers could not serve as a primary reference for Apple's tablet, the iPad, even though earlier tablets had several ornamental features in common with the iPad. The trial court found that a previous tablet computer had, like the iPad, four rounded corners, a flat glass-like surface without any ornamentation, and an overall design that conveys thinness, thereby creating "basically the same visual impression" and rendering the iPad design unpatentable for obviousness. The Federal Circuit disagreed, explaining that despite these striking similarities, various differences, including a greater contrast between the screen and the rest of the older tablet, meant that the older tablet could not serve as a primary reference for the iPad.[13] Without a primary reference, the game was up: Apple's design patent had to be considered nonobvious, paving the way for its massive infringement verdict against rival Samsung. The *Apple* trial court notwithstanding, courts rarely identify works exhibiting the necessary degree of similarity to the patentee's design to be a primary reference. The same holds true for examiners at the PTO.[14]

Holistic Evaluation

As it demands a nearly identical primary reference, the Federal Circuit also insists that the "ordinary designer" approaches her work in a holistic manner. This means that instead of giving greater attention to design aspects that might be more noticeable or important to consumers, designers (and, by extension, judges and juries) take in everything at once. In other words, all design elements are created equal.

This design agnosticism is gospel when it comes to comparing the claimed work to the prior art. "[T]here are no portions of a design which are 'immaterial' or 'not important'," explained the Federal Circuit's predecessor. "A design is a unitary thing and all of its portions are material in that they contribute to the appearance which constitutes the design."[15] More recent decisions insist only "the visual impressions of the designs as a whole" can be considered, not "selected, separate features of the prior art."[16] Judges must be cautious even when describing what they see as "[l]isting details of ornamentation is an inappropriate construction because it does not project the overall visual impression of the design."[17]

This insistence that no one part of a design is more important than another might sound like it would make nonobviousness harder to prove, thereby making it more difficult to claim a valid design patent. Things can look more similar the less detailed your perspective is. If courts can only take a broad view of the entire design, then it might be harder to point out differences between the claimed design and the prior art necessary for a finding of nonobviousness.

In actuality, however, by assuming that designers approach design holistically, the Federal Circuit has made it easier to show nonobviousness. If one detail cannot be prioritized over another, then *any* detail becomes a potential difference from the prior art – a difference that prevents an earlier design from serving as the necessary primary reference. As discussed, in the *Apple* case, the Federal Circuit second-guessed the trial judge's determination that another tablet possessed the same key stylistic features as Apple's iPad. The Federal Circuit noted differences that it said made the iPad design nonobvious, but it made no effort to explain why the differences it pointed out were more important than the similarities identified by the district court. The importance or materiality of a particular design feature to the designer (or to consumers) is not part of the nonobviousness analysis, which makes it all the easier for the design patent holder to find at least one legally sufficient difference between its creation and what came before. Even features not visible to onlookers at the point of sale are now considered potential grounds for distinguishing the prior art and declaring a design nonobvious.[18]

THE FALSE ART–SCIENCE DICHOTOMY

The reason for such an anemic approach to nonobviousness is a belief that interrogation of design inventiveness cannot lend itself to a specific analysis and is, in fact, "impossible."[19] Even the court with the most expertise on this question, the Federal Circuit, confesses that it is necessarily flying blind. Considering the obviousness of the design of Crocs shoes, the Federal Circuit acknowledged its own lack of discernment: "Courts, made up of laymen as they must be, are likely either to underrate, or to overrate, the difficulties in making new and profitable discoveries in fields with which they cannot be familiar."[20]

Without objective criteria to apply, courts are left to rely largely on their own subjective sense to evaluate nonobviousness. "The essence of a design has been said to reside," explains one patent authority, "not in the elements individually, but to exist in that indefinable whole that awakens some sensation in the observer's mind."[21] An oft-repeated statement of the law dating back to 1900 emphasizes the indescribable nature of a design's effect on viewers, the exact area of study for nonobviousness:

> Design, in the view of the patent law, is that characteristic of a physical substance which, by means of lines, images, configuration, and the like, taken as a whole, makes an impression, through the eye upon the mind of the observer. The essence of a design resides, not in the elements individually, nor in their method of arrangement, but in their tout ensemble – in that indefinable whole that awakens some sensation in the observer's mind.[22]

The Federal Circuit instructs that a "trial judge may determine almost *instinctively* whether the two designs create basically the same visual impression."[23]

The design process is so magical and individualized, in the courts' eyes, that even attempting to discuss their own observation of a design is problematic. Although courts are required to provide some sort of account of their nonobviousness determinations, there is a skepticism as to how such a determination can be articulated into textual or even rational terms: "Words are often an inadequate substitute for the overall visual impression created upon the observer of the item at issue compared to that of its alleged predecessors."[24] Given this belief that the design process is unknowable, one can understand why the Federal Circuit prohibits inquiries into the materiality of particular design features and adopts a test for nonobviousness that only involves the simplistic analysis of looking for a single design virtually identical to the claimed design.

Courts hearing copyright cases often follow a similar path, refusing to examine what came before to probe a work's innovative force. Take the decision of a federal appellate court to award copyright in "a rectangular object having a stone-like appearance and a verse inscribed on the face." Even though the verse was copied word for word from the public domain, the court of appeals deemed the object original, giving the author creative credit for presenting the verse in a particular font and capitalizing the first letter of each word. The court offered no comparison to other garden sculptures or sculptures in general to support its decision that the author had added "her own imaginative spark" to the work.[25] Along similar lines, another appellate court concluded that the not "particularly novel" face, lips, and eyes of Barbie dolls were copyrightable, brushing aside a trial court determination that similar features already existed in many other dolls. The court proclaimed even if there were many other dolls with "upturned noses, bow lips, and wide-spread eyes," this should not prevent Barbie and her "current sales exceed[ing] $1 billion per year" from enjoying copyright protection.[26]

As with design patent law, if a judge hearing a copyright matter strays by comparing a work to the relevant prior art and finding insufficient difference, she can be reprimanded. When a federal court departed from the norm and determined that a photograph of a Skyy vodka bottle against a plain white background lacked adequate creativity, it was reversed by a court of appeals. The lower court compared the photograph to the original bottle, finding the photograph insufficiently creative because any differences between the original bottle and the version in the photograph would be undetectable to a jury. Rather than approving the lower court's comparison of the photograph against the most important item of prior art – the bottle itself – the appellate court faulted the district court for ignoring precedent holding that almost any photograph is per se creative.[27]

But if both copyright law and design patent law fail to rigorously engage with prior art to assess creativity, it is at least possible for judges hearing copyright cases to sometimes consider prior works in their determinations. Copyright law has no "primary reference" requirement – for a finding of insufficient creativity, it is not necessary to locate a single existing work that is exactly the same as the would-be author's work. If the expressive features of a work can all be attributed to a *combination* of features from other, pre-existing works, then the work is not original and cannot be copyrighted.[28] By contrast, thanks to the Federal Circuit's primary reference requirement, if there is no single existing design that is "virtually identical" to the claimed design, then all previous designs become irrelevant, even if, in combination, they feature all of the same elements as the claimed design.

Design patent law's narrow approach to nonobviousness stands in marked contrast to utility patent law, which calls for a probing inquiry into whether an invention represents a sufficiently inventive leap from what came before. Unlike their investigation of design patent matters, courts hearing utility patent cases insist that the nonobviousness standard demands objective evaluation, tethering the requirement to various information about other works in the relevant domain. The scope and content of relevant prior art, the level of ordinary skill in the prior art, the differences between the claimed invention and the prior art, and the invention's role in resolving long felt but unsolved needs are all part of the utility patent nonobviousness inquiry. Rather than insisting on a single reference nearly equivalent to the claimed invention, in utility patent cases, a court is expected to combine multiple references to see if their combination would have been apparent to a person skilled in the art. For example, a packaging device that injects air into a horizontal stack of bags and holds them in place with a pin was considered obvious in light of other packaging devices accomplishing the same end but with vertical stacks and rods instead of pins.[29] To meet utility patent law's creativity threshold, the inventor must truly distinguish herself from what has come before instead of making a single minor deviation.

The very different treatment of design and utility patent nonobviousness demonstrates a belief that visual art and scientific invention represent two different mental phenomena. The former cannot be appreciated by outsiders and can only be evaluated, if at all, through instinct. The latter represents a rational, calculated process that invariably relies on previous innovations and can be meticulously analyzed according to objective criteria. This art/science double standard has consequences: the PTO initially rejects nearly 90 percent of all utility patent applications at the same time that it approves 90 percent of all design patent applications, and the differential does not improve when one considers the nonobviousness analysis of the federal courts.[30]

ALL CREATIVITY REQUIRES CONTEXT

Psychologists once had a similar view as to the gulf between artistic and scientific creativity. They divided all creativity into lower- and higher-level processes, placing achievement in the arts at the highest level. Today, however, the consensus is that "artistic creativity may not hold a privileged place in the brain after all."[31] By observing the same neural phenomena in different kinds of creative tasks, researchers reject old beliefs that divided artistic and scientific creativity into separate camps.

Relatedly, the once widely accepted theory that people are divided into two cognitive tribes – creative, right-brained, free-spirited artists and analytical, left-brained, math/science-oriented logicians – has been thoroughly discredited, even if this conceit still finds its way into popular discourse.[32] It turns out that inventors are no less creative than artists. The supposedly non-creative left hemisphere of the brain is actively involved in all manner of creative tasks.[33] For engineers as well as poets, the same process takes place: coming up with an idea, then building on that idea so that it is useful. This process requires both sides of the brain to be engaged. To the extent design patent law depends on a view of creativity in visual design as different in kind from other creative thought processes, neuroscience shows this view to be mistaken.[34]

What the science reveals about the creative process is the importance of domain-specific knowledge – chiefly knowledge of the prior art – no matter the discipline. Instead of finding differences between creative thought in the arts and the sciences, researchers posit a dual model of creativity with all creators cycling between idea generation and evaluation of ideas against a benchmark of standards.[35] To learn these standards, it helps to have training in the domain. "Creative people are generally very knowledgeable about a given discipline. Coming up with a grand idea without ever having been closely involved with an area of study is not impossible, but it is very improbable."[36] It is important to know the norms, techniques, and history of your chosen artistic field before you create. Even for those who seek to break boundaries, it is good to know what you are breaking.

The law of design nonobviousness looks to the designer alone, but creativity must be understood as existing in a larger framework beyond the individual creator. As the psychologist Mikhail Csikszentmihalyi explains it, "an idea or product that deserves the label 'creative' arises from the synergy of many sources and not only from the mind of a single person." According to Csikszentmihalyi's influential systems model of the creative process, creativity emerges from a dynamic interaction of three elements: (1) the individual: the person (or persons) that produces the creative work; (2) the domain: an area of specialized knowledge; and (3) the field: the hierarchy of people and groups who possess deep knowledge of the domain and act as its gatekeepers.[37] Other creativity models build on the essential insights of the systems model, such as its emphasis on the need to consider the prior art of each relevant domain and the role of the domain's anointed experts.

It is only recently that psychologists have gained a markedly better understanding of the creative process so that these models can actually be tested. Though by no means offering a complete map of the creative process, neural measurements confirm the broad outlines of the systems model. At the individual level, as discussed in the previous chapter, motivation to create turns out to be of central importance for creative activity and accidental production of innovative works rare. But creativity can only be understood by also looking beyond the individual to the larger creative environment. A flood of experiments show that creativity requires a comparison between the expressive product at issue and the past work and shared practices of the relevant artistic community. Without this domain-specific referent, the systems model explains, there is no basis for determining what is creative and what is not. This is why highly creative people tend to be creative in one particular domain instead of several; "it takes a lot of experience, knowledge, and training to be able to identify good problems."[38]

This is not to say that creativity is only a matter of directly applying domain-specific expertise. An innovative designer still needs to find ways to combine elements in new formations that are not obvious or conventional. But domain-specific knowledge is critical to creative success. Without first learning what has already been done, a person doesn't have the raw material to create with. That's why a critical part of the creative process is to first become very familiar with prior works, and internalize the symbols and conventions of the domain.[39] A good illustration of this comes from the world of automotive design. Many of the most important car designs of the past century – from Cadillac's introduction of tail fins to the retro look of Chrysler's PT Cruiser – owe significant debts to earlier automotive styling cues, either as a point of departure or a planned homage.[40]

Even though domain-specific expertise is essential for visual creativity, as it is for all other kinds of creativity, it is typically ignored when judging the patentability of a design. Rather than examining the relevant universe of prior art in the domain and comparing it against the design at issue, courts can dispense with nonobviousness through a simplistic look for the claimed design's identical twin. This search for a single overlapping reference is problematic. It does not align with what we now understand about the creative process, particularly the great importance of familiarity with relevant prior art to that process. Tellingly, there is no primary reference requirement when it comes to determining utility patent nonobviousness, thus revealing a double standard in patent law's treatment of science versus visual art.[41] Chapter 4 offers more detail on how prior art can be evaluated in a way that resembles the creative process and generates a more rigorous screen for design patent nonobviousness.

Notes

1 U.S. Patent No. D48,160 (Nov. 16, 1915).
2 U.S. Patent No. D11,023 (Feb. 18, 1879).
3 Egyptian Goddess, Inc. v. Swisa, Inc., 543 F.3d 665 (Fed. Cir. 2008) (eliminating old requirement that the accused device contain substantially the same points of novelty that distinguished the patented design from the

prior art; now the accused design must only appear "substantially similar" to that patented design to the "ordinary observer"); Jury Verdict, Apple, Inc. v. Samsung Elecs. Co., No. 11-CV-01846-LHK (May 24, 2018), ECF No. 3806 (approving jury award of $533 million for Samsung's infringement of Apple's design patents).

4 Walter E. Durling v. Spectrum Furniture Co., 101 F.3d 100, 103 (Fed. Cir. 1996).

5 Litton Systems, Inc. v. Whirlpool Corp., 728 F.2d 1423, 1441 (Fed. Cir. 1984).

6 Hon. Giles S. Rich, *Laying the Ghost of the 'Invention' Requirement*, 1 AIPLA Q.J. 26 (1972).

7 U.S. CONST. art I, § 8, cl. 8.

8 Laura G. Pedraza-Fariña & Ryan Whalen, *A Network Theory of Patentability*, 87 U. CHI. L. REV. 63, 65 (2020).

9 MRC Innovations, Inc. v. Hunter Mfg., 747 F.3d 1326, 1331 (Fed. Cir. 2014).

10 Titan Tire Corp. v. Case New Holland, Inc., 566 F.3d 1372, 1381 (Fed. Cir. 2009).

11 Campbell Soup Co. v. Gamon Plus, Inc., 939 F.3d 1335, 1339 (Fed. Cir. 2019).

12 *In re* Leon Rosen, 673 F.2d 388, 391 (C.C.P.A. 1982).

13 Apple, Inc. v. Samsung Elecs. Co., 678 F.3d 1314, 1331–32 (Fed. Cir. 2012).

14 Sarah Burstein, *Is Design Patent Examination Too Lax?*, 33 BERKELEY TECH. L.J. 607, 616–17 (2018).

15 *In re* Blum, 153 U.S.P.Q. 177, 179–80 (C.C.P.A. 1967).

16 *In re* Harvey, 12 F.3d 1061, 1065 (Fed. Cir. 1993).

17 Ashley Furniture Indus., Inc. v. Lifestyle Enter., Inc., 574 F. Supp. 2d 920, 928 (W.D. Wisc. 2008). See also Titan Tire Corp. v. Case New Holland, Inc., 566 F.3d 1372, 1383 (Fed. Cir. 2009) (cautioning against "the tendency to draw the court's attention to individual features of a design rather than the design's overall appearance").

18 Contessa Food Products, Inc. v. Conagra, Inc., 282 F.3d 1370, 1381 (Fed. Cir. 2002).

19 Judge Giles Rich, the "dean" of the Federal Circuit, referred to "obviousness in design patentability cases" as the "impossible issue." *In re* Nalbandian, 661 F.2d 1214, 1219 (C.C.P.A. 1981) (Rich, J., concurring).

20 Crocs, Inc. v. ITC, 598 F.3d 1294, 1310 (Fed. Cir. 2010) (quoting Safety Car Heating & Lightning Co. v. Gen. Elec. Co., 155 F.2d 937, 939 (2d Cir. 1946)).

21 3 JOHN GLADSTONE MILLS ET AL., PATENT LAW FUNDAMENTALS § 8:5 (2d ed. 2020).

[22] Application of Zahn, 617 F.2d 261, 270 (C.C.P.A. 1980) (Baldwin, J., dissenting) (quoting Pelouze Scale & Mfg. Co. v. American Cutlery Co., 102 F. 916, 918 (7th Cir. 1900)).

[23] Spigen Korea Co. v. Ultraproof, Inc., 955 F.3d 1379, 1383–84 (Fed. Cir. 2020) (quoting Durling v. Spectrum Furniture Co., 101 F.3d 100, 103 (Fed. Cir. 1996)) (emphasis added).

[24] Thomas B. Lindgren, *The Sanctity of the Design Patent: Illusion or Reality? Twenty Years of Design Patent Litigation Since* Compco v. Day-Brite Lighting, Inc. *and* Sears, Roebuck & Co. v. Stiffel Co., 10 OKLA. CITY U. L. REV. 195, 225 (1985).

[25] Kay Berry, Inc. v. Taylor Gifts, Inc., 421 F.3d 199, 207 (3d Cir. 2005).

[26] Mattel, Inc. v. Goldberger Doll Mfg. Co., 365 F.3d 133, 135 (2d Cir. 2004).

[27] Ets-Hokin v. Skyy Spirits, Inc., 225 F.3d 1068, 1077 (9th Cir. 2000).

[28] Copyright law does offer limited protection to compilations involving the creative selection or arrangement of elements that would be uncopyrightable on their own. See Feist Publ'ns v. Rural Tele. Serv. Co., 499 U.S. 340, 348 (1991).

[29] *In re* Winslow, 365 F.2d 1017 (C.C.P.A. 1966).

[30] Burstein, *supra*, at 610; Vic Lin, *Design Patents vs Utility Patents: What Are the Differences?*, PATENT TRADEMARK BLOG, https://www.patenttrademarkblog.com/design-patents-vs-utility-patents-differences/. When amended patent applications responding to an initial disallowance are considered, the utility patent allowance rate reaches 55 percent – still far below the 90 percent allowance rate for design patents. Michael Carley et al., *What Is the Probability of Receiving a U.S. Patent?*, 17 YALE J.L. & TECH. 203, 209 (2015).

[31] Malinda J. McPherson & Charles J. Limb, *Artistic and Aesthetic Production: Progress and Limitations, in* CAMBRIDGE HANDBOOK OF THE NEUROSCIENCE OF CREATIVITY 517, 524 (Rex E. Jung & Oshin Vartanian eds. 2018).

[32] Allison B. Kaufman et al., *The Neurobiological Foundation of Creative Cognition, in* CAMBRIDGE HANDBOOK OF CREATIVITY 216, 219 (James C. Kaufman & Robert J. Sternberg eds. 2010).

[33] A. R. Aghababyan et al., EEG REACTIONS DURING CREATIVE ACTIVITY, 33 HUMAN PHYSIOLOGY 252, 252–53 (2007). See also Arne Dietrich & Riam Kanso, *A Review of EEG, ERP, and Neuroimaging Studies of Creativity and Insight*, 136 PSYCH. BULL. 822, 825 (2010) (cataloging EEG studies of divergent thinking to show that the notion of lateralized brain creativity is unsubstantiated for either side of the brain).

[34] Jared A. Nielsen et al., *An Evaluation of the Left Brain vs. Right Brain Hypothesis with Resting State Functional Connectivity Magnetic Resonance Imaging*, 8 PLOS ONE e712275 (2013).

[35] Oded M. Kleinmintz et al., *The Twofold Model of Creativity: The Neural Underpinnings of the Generation and Evaluation of Creative Ideas*, 27 CURRENT OP. BEHAV. SCI. 131, 131 (2019).

[36] Ulrich Kraft, *Unleashing Creativity*, 16 SCIENTIFIC AMERICAN MIND 21, 22 (2005). See also Carlos Blanco, *Philosophy, Neuroscience, and the Gift of Creativity*, 1 REVISTA ARGUMENTA 95, 108 (2017) (contending that "knowledge of the present status of a certain discipline ... underlie[s] the great triumphs of human creativity").

[37] MIHALY CSIKSZENTMIHALYI, CREATIVITY: FLOW AND THE PSYCHOLOGY OF DISCOVERY AND INVENTION 6 (1996).

[38] R. KEITH SAWYER, EXPLAINING CREATIVITY: THE SCIENCE OF HUMAN INNOVATION 65 (2d ed. 2012).

[39] *Id.* at 93.

[40] Larry Printz, *The Rise and Fall (and Rise Again) of Retro Car Design*, ARS TECHNICA, Jan. 15, 2021.

[41] Another problem with the primary reference rule is that it conflates the nonobviousness and novelty requirements, making one of them superfluous. In interpreting legislation, courts are meant to avoid redundancy by construing potentially overlapping terms to have independent meanings. See Lutheran Day Care v. Snohomish Cnty., 829 P.2d 746, 751–52 (Wash. 1992) ("Statutes should not be interpreted in such a manner as to render any portion meaningless, superfluous, or questionable").

PART II

Understanding Audiences for Art and Advertising

3 NEUROAESTHETICS AND COPYRIGHT INFRINGEMENT

Jimi Hendrix first met fifteen-year-old guitarist Randy Wolfe in a New York City music store in 1966. After some talking and jamming together, the as-yet-unknown Hendrix invited Wolfe (whom he dubbed "Randy California") to sit in with his band. Shortly thereafter, the two had a falling out. Hendrix moved on to superstardom. Wolfe formed a band named Spirit that had some success, including a top-40 hit. But he never quite cracked the big time like Hendrix.

Wolfe died in a drowning accident in 1997, but his music lives on in many ways, including in the form of an epic legal clash with iconic rock band Led Zeppelin. Wolfe's estate sued Led Zeppelin for copyright infringement, contending that Led Zeppelin's rock anthem "Stairway to Heaven" copied key portions of Wolfe's song "Taurus." "Stairway to Heaven" is often rated the greatest rock song of all time, enjoying more sheet music sales and radio play than virtually any other musical composition. The lawyer for Wolfe's estate estimated that his lawsuit against Led Zeppelin was worth $40 million.

The *Led Zeppelin* case exemplifies many of the frustrations courts and commentators have with the current state of copyright infringement law. Not everything in a song is copyrightable. Commentators fretted that the California jury hearing the case would base its decision on uncopyrightable stock motifs appearing in both works. The jury was instructed to determine "whether the ordinary, reasonable person would find the total concept and feel of the works to be substantially similar."[1] It ultimately found in Led Zeppelin's favor, but one might wonder whether a different group of listeners – perhaps ones with more musical expertise or more familiarity with 1970s rock and roll – would have a different reaction to the two songs and reach an entirely different verdict.

Creativity is not the only area of copyright law that could benefit from further definition. As the *Led Zeppelin* case illustrates, the test for copyright infringement offers little guidance or predictability for litigants. Even in high stakes cases, the trier of fact's analysis of whether one work infringes another remains largely unknowable and underdetermined. The problem largely lies in the decision to make a particular kind of audience reaction the centerpiece of copyright infringement without any corresponding way to ascertain the inputs that make up that reaction. One might think that every copyright jury should be instructed in how to appreciate the perspective of the relevant audience for the work at issue. Instead, the *Led Zeppelin* jury, like all triers of fact in copyright infringement disputes, faced the daunting task of trying to recreate an audience's experience with creative works with no tools for understanding that experience save their own personal responses to those works. As the appellate court hearing the *Led Zeppelin* case affirmed, the substantial similarity analysis demands a "subjective" comparison of the two works, seemingly closing the door on any attempts to more precisely identify what an audience for Wolfe's work would find most relevant when comparing it to "Stairway to Heaven."[2]

This chapter details the centrality of audience understanding to the test for copyright infringement and how neuroscience can facilitate that understanding. Neuroaesthetics – the study of the neural processes underlying aesthetic appreciation – challenges some longstanding principles of copyright law, including the law's refusal to distinguish between different audiences and its insistence on the inherent subjectivity of aesthetic pleasure. History is important here; by seeing how the law changed over time, we can better appreciate the assumptions about audiences embedded in the test for copyright infringement.

THE ROLE OF THE AUDIENCE IN COPYRIGHT LAW

Copyright's early history reflected a belief that judges could evaluate similarity on their own terms and that their study of the works at issue did not need to be filtered through the gaze of an audience. In the early twentieth century, courts confidently determined when "the same impressions will be created, and the same emotions excited" by two works.[3] Substantial similarity could be assessed without regard for audience sensibilities. Instead, the task of the judge was to simply compare the works and determine if the defendant had borrowed too heavily from the plaintiff. This permitted the judge to engage in an exacting scrutiny of the two works; there was no need to avoid such scrutiny out of concern that this was not the way the works would be processed by their actual audience. Rather than fearing that they were not representative of the larger population, judges believed their eyes and ears were as good if not better than those of ordinary listeners and considered this sensory superiority an advantage in deciding infringement cases.

An early illustrative example comes from the case of *Sheldon* v. *Metro-Goldwyn Pictures Corp*. The trial judge in that matter justified his refusal to trust the audience's perspective over his own as well as his decision that a film was not substantially similar to the plaintiff's play this way:

> I must, as the trier of the facts, have a more Olympian viewpoint than the average playgoer. I must look at the two opposing productions, the Play and the Picture, not only comparatively, but, as it were, genealogically.[4]

In review, an appellate court disagreed with the judge's take, but simply replaced one "Olympian viewpoint" with another, opining that it knew infringement had occurred because "the dramatic significance of the scenes [in the two works] is the same, almost to the letter."[5]

The trial judge's temerity to nakedly assert the right to decide the case from his particular perspective and the appellate court's willingness to interpose its own view stands in sharp contrast to the modern instruction that substantial similarity must be evaluated through the senses of the ordinary observer. Most trace the arrival of the ordinary observer test to the case of *Arnstein* v. *Porter*. Though drawing on strands of earlier case law that highlighted the perspective of the audience, *Arnstein* cemented the move to determine infringement based on the impressions of an ordinary audience member, a doctrinal innovation that has achieved "canonical status" in copyright jurisprudence.[6]

Ira Arnstein was a musical composer with a paranoid streak. In the 1930s and 1940s he launched a wave of copyright infringement lawsuits against various well-known composers and publishers. His complaints against these musical luminaries not only alleged infringement of his compositions, but other provocative allegations. In 1945, he filed a lawsuit against famed composer and songwriter Cole Porter. Not only had Porter wrongfully appropriated his musical works, Arnstein contended, but he had also hired "stooges to follow me, watch me, and live in the same apartment with me."[7]

Porter moved for a pretrial disposal of the case, which was granted by a federal district court. Arnstein appealed the district court's decision to the Second Circuit Court of Appeals where it was heard by a trio of legal legends: Judges Jerome Frank, Learned Hand, and Charles Clark. Frank's importance to American copyright law was discussed in Chapter 1. Clark had been the dean of Yale Law School. Hand is one of the most influential judges in United States history, having been quoted by legal scholars and the US Supreme Court more than any other lower-court judge. This august panel reversed the district court, asserting that there were two parts to every infringement analysis – (1) whether the defendant copied from the protected work (i.e., "copying in fact") and (2) whether such copying constituted "improper appropriation" – and both were questions of fact that needed to proceed to trial if there was "the slightest doubt."[8] Writing for the majority, Judge Frank considered it to still be an open question as to whether Porter could have copied Arnstein's work, even if some of his allegations rang fantastic. Frank also explained that the issue of improper appropriation (what we now call "substantial similarity") could not be disposed of as neatly as the district court wished. A jury or judge must decide this issue from the vantage point of an "ordinary lay hearer," something that had not been done at the trial court level. Frank even suggested that a jury – so long as "tone-deaf persons" were excluded from it – would be better at this task than out-of-touch judges unfamiliar with popular music and that, in the advent of a bench trial, a judge trying such a case should solicit the input of an advisory jury.

Before *Arnstein*, being able to filter out unprotectable elements from consideration was considered more important to evaluating substantial similarity than conveying the audience's overall reaction to the work. The *Sheldon* judge asserted the superiority of his "Olympian" perspective over what the plaintiff's attorney urged, which was to consider "the impression of the Play and the Picture on the 'average playgoer'" in a way analogous to "the reasonable man in other branches of the law."[9] The judge explained that because both works were based on the same public domain element free to all to use – a mid-nineteenth-century trial – it made more sense to decide the case based on an objective, legally adept perspective that could filter out uncopyrightable similarities. After *Arnstein*, priorities flipped: it was now considered more important to identify the impressions of the target audience than to worry about the risk that those impressions might rely on unprotectable ideas or expressive material from the public domain.

Today, every federal court evaluates substantial similarity from the perspective of a lay audience. Even when a judge (instead of a jury) decides the issue of infringement, she is meant to do so through the eyes and ears of the audience for the work. *Arnstein*'s push to make the infringement analysis revolve around audience impressions had two primary consequences.

First, expert witnesses could not be used to inform an infringement analysis dependent on the perceptions of laypersons. If the intended audience for a work is one with an ordinary eye and ordinary ear for literature, music, or visual art, then the opinions of experts with extraordinary artistic sensibilities arguably offer no insight and might even bias a trier of fact trying to guess the reactions of that audience. As a result, courts since *Arnstein* have largely blocked expert testimony on the question of substantial similarity. In some jurisdictions, there is an outright prohibition on expert assistance in the substantial similarity analysis.

Second, once the perspective of the ordinary observer became paramount, copyright infringement claims could rarely be disposed of before trial. After all, if the infringement analysis depended on an assessment of what "is recognizable by an ordinary observer,"[10] then it would seem inappropriate for the judge to substitute her opinion on infringement for that of the lay juror. Recognizing the new paradigm, appellate judges warned lower court judges away from making pretrial judgments based on their own comparison of the plaintiff's and defendant's works. As one early opinion following *Arnstein* chastised, judges who award summary judgment to defendants "when upon a reading of the two works it seems unlikely from their relative merits that the common matter could have been borrowed . . . deprive the plaintiff of his day in court."[11] Judgment on the issue of substantial similarity before trial continues to be disfavored. As explained by the federal court of appeals with jurisdiction over California cases, "subjective comparisons of literary works that are objectively similar in their expression of ideas must be left to the trier of fact."[12]

A final critical point is that the substantial similarity analysis is premised on the assumption that different audiences will react to creative works in the same way. The *Arnstein* decision holds that triers of fact need to experience the works at issue subjectively, without the intrusion of expert testimony or instructions to dissect and compare the works' individual components. Yet the decision also assumes that this subjective process will lead to common conclusions instead of each juror coming up with their own idiosyncratic analysis. Otherwise, jurors should be precluded from determining substantial similarity. One might worry that one audience member's reaction is likely to differ from another, causing infringement decisions to vary based on the personal predilections of individual judges and jurors, particularly when these decisions are not kept in check through judicial or expert guidance. Instead, it is assumed that the trier of fact can uncover the aesthetic essence bound up in a creative work in a way that translates across audiences and does not require specialized training.

Reflecting this belief in a largely universal aesthetic experience, courts rarely consider the views of a particular audience. Most decisions fall back on the presumption that "the response of the ordinary reasonable person" will serve as an adequate stand-in for the target audience. Jury instructions vary between asking jurors to determine whether an "ordinary reasonable person" would find the works substantially similar to equating the concept of the ordinary reasonable observer with the jurors themselves. The implication seems to be that jurors are a sufficient proxy for the audience because they will have the same ultimate response to the two works as that audience. "In most cases, when a copyrighted work will be directed at the public in general, the court need only apply a general public formulation to the intended audience test."[13]

Perhaps because of this belief in aesthetic universality, courts reject opportunities to use outside evidence to gain a better understanding of audience differences. Surveys of representative audience members are not admissible in copyright infringement actions. Take, for example, a case involving the manufacture of action figures thought to resemble characters from the first *Star Wars* film. An effort to introduce a survey of the perceptions of children – the relevant audience for these creative works – was rebuffed. The court explained that admitting such a survey would set the "dangerous precedent of allowing trial by the court to be replaced by public opinion poll."[14] Similarly, in a different matter involving a television show alleged to infringe the "Superman" character, a court blocked consideration of survey evidence out of concern such evidence would usurp what should be the trier of fact's independent role in determining substantial similarity.[15]

Contrast this state of affairs with the widespread use of outside evidence of audience perception in the related field of trademark law. Courts have been much more transparent about their own difficulties in accurately assessing the minds of consumers in trademark cases. As a result, the history of trademark law reveals a growing acceptance of outside evidence to determine issues of likely consumer confusion as well as mark distinctiveness. Survey evidence is widely accepted and even required for some of trademark law's legal questions. For trademark infringement claims, courts deploy multi-factor tests to determine the likelihood of consumer confusion from the defendant's activities. All of these tests call for consideration of evidence of "actual confusion" – whether in the form of survey evidence or anecdotal testimony – and "customer sophistication," which allows for scrutiny of the particularized understandings of the relevant target consuming group. In sum, there is a much greater willingness to solicit outside aid to understand a target audience when it comes to that audience's processing of brand names and symbols than when it comes to an audience's encounters with music and literature.

RESPECTING AUDIENCE DIFFERENCE

By characterizing the audience members' experience of creative works as both subjective and universal, the current test for copyright infringement matches the view of the most important philosopher of aesthetics:

Immanuel Kant. Writing in the eighteenth-century, Kant referred to aesthetic judgment as "the judgment of taste," and explained that the experience of pleasure from art had a necessarily "subjective condition."[16] But Kant also insisted on the commonality, or what he described as the "universal validity," of aesthetic encounters. As he explained, "if [someone] proclaims something to be beautiful, then he requires the same liking from others; he then judges not just for himself but for everyone, and speaks of beauty as if it were a property of things."[17] Agreeing with this folk intuition about our responses to art, Kant maintained that aesthetic judgments are like empirical judgments (e.g., there are ten provinces in Canada) in that they claim universal validity, although they are different from empirical judgments in that they are made on the basis of an inner subjective response. In accord with Kant, copyright's infringement analysis relies on the assumption that audience members respond to creative works in their own way but somehow arrive at common conclusions.

Neuroaesthetic research challenges this assumption. A great deal of this research reveals audience difference. For example, brain imaging demonstrates differences in how men and women process art and how they experience music.[18] Imagine a copyright infringement dispute involving a work consumed predominantly by one gender. Consider fan fiction. Although fan fiction is diverse and different works and genres in fan fiction can have different readerships, most fan fiction is written by women and its audience trends female. If women experience fan fiction differently from men, an analysis of substantial similarity without attention to this difference risks either over- or under-policing copyright in a discriminatory manner.

In judging substantial similarity, the law assumes not only that people will respond to the same works in the same ways but that this aesthetic experience stays the same regardless of prior experience with the work's style, genre, or format. Neuroscience offers the ability to compare the aesthetic responses of audiences with different backgrounds and search for differences in their reactions. Studies reveal cognitive differences in the ways experts and non-experts react to creative works. Some amount of artistic training produces changes in "art-specific organization in the cerebellum."[19] As expertise increases so does visual exploration of a painting's overall composition, background features, and color contrasts. The "art-naïve," however, spend more time looking at individual figurative elements and figures in the painting's center and foreground.[20] Along similar lines, a comparison of the brain activity of architects and non-architects revealed that only the architects retrieved information stored in memory when assessing the aesthetic appeal of different buildings.[21]

The research shows that familiarity inevitably influences perception. Experience triggers more attention to technique and style when rendering an aesthetic judgment; lack of experience prompts greater reliance on personal feelings.[22] Audiences differ wildly in their familiarity with different art forms. For example, there is a wide disparity among the general population in terms of musical experience. This means that one jury or judge will likely have significantly different aesthetic responses from another. It is not that some audience members are comfortable evaluating creative works and others are not. Everyone makes aesthetic judgments, even if they lack training or familiarity with the category of work at issue. It is just that the means and content of these judgments differ based on who is making the judgment and their background relationship to the work.

Regardless of audience familiarity, the process of aesthetic judgment changes depending on the kind of artistic work at issue. Abstract art prompts more varied aesthetic reactions than representational art.[23] Dance expertise exhibits its own unique biology.[24] Perhaps most significantly, our biological responses to visual works differ from our responses to aural ones.[25] For example, there is evidence that listeners perceive music in a dissective manner as they analyze various individual features of a song rather than evaluating the song holistically. By contrast, evaluation of other creative works involves a more gestalt-like analysis.[26]

Copyright law ignores these differences in audience evaluation that depend on the mode of creative expression. The infringement analysis remains the same regardless of the kind of creative work at issue or the particular senses employed to appreciate that art. Courts generally avoid adjusting to differences in creative formats, instead assuming that aesthetic judgment operates in the same fashion in one artistic context as it does in the other. Neuroscience shows that this assumption is false and that it effects legal outcomes. For example, the difference between the aesthetic processing of visual and aural works has direct implications for music infringement cases. Such cases can hinge upon a judge's choice to believe that the relevant audience will either consider a song in its entirety or focus its attention on a particular measure in the work's chorus.

Some might question whether neuroaesthetic research, which, by necessity, is conducted with small sample sizes, can offer generalizable insights into the reactions of large audiences. Can a study of less than fifty people really reveal the aesthetic preferences and behaviors of thousands? The answer is that, in a variety of contexts, small sample sizes for neuroscientific studies supply results that apply to larger, legally relevant populations. Although there is variability, "studies of aesthetic preference are reasonably consistent in their findings."[27] Instead of being hopelessly different, aesthetic reactions *in particular audiences* appear to have enough coherence that information about these reactions can help inform copyright's effort to understand audiences. Keep in mind that, in the context of copyright infringement, everyone in a target audience need not evaluate an artwork in the same way for such evidence to be probative. A finding of substantial similarity relies only on general agreement about the audience's aesthetic experience, not certitude about the uniformity of that experience.

Hence, neuroaesthetic research challenges copyright's assumption that most audiences think alike. This research demonstrates that there are enough differences in aesthetic judgment to invalidate copyright's one-size-fits-all approach to audience reaction. The mechanics of aesthetic judgment change depending on the modality of creative expression. Unfortunately, copyright law offers no guidance to a trier of fact striving to understand audience difference. Nor, as described below, does it offer much direction for comprehending how any audience member is likely to render an aesthetic judgment.

UNDERSTANDING AESTHETIC APPEAL

In 2009, Tashera Simmons came up with an idea for a reality show called "Hip Hop Wives." Simmons was married to the rapper DMX, but a string of arrests and extra-marital affairs took their toll on the relationship, and the pair ultimately divorced. Simmons envisioned a show about the trials and tribulations of women, including herself, in relationships with hip hop artists. She pitched the idea to the television network VH1. VH1 passed, but two years later began airing a reality show called "Love & Hip Hop" focused on the personal and professional lives of women in the hip hop industry. The show grew into a major media franchise with over 350 episodes airing to generally high ratings.

There were a number of similarities between the "Hip Hop Wives" proposal and the first season of "Love & Hip Hop." Both shows centered on the troubled personal relationships of women attached in some form to the hip hop industry. Both featured Chrissy Lampkin, partner of the hip-hop artist Jim Jones. Both shows were described as having a "fast" and "high-octane" pace. Nevertheless, a court concluded that "no reasonable jury could conclude that the two works are substantially similar."[28]

Three years earlier, the same court needed to decide another copyright infringement suit involving reality television. This time, the plaintiff managed to convince the court that a jury could find the two works substantially similar. The plaintiff proposed a reality show that pitted celebrity contestants against one another in events designed to mimic the training for Navy Seals. A producer affiliated with NBCUniversal responded favorably to the plaintiff's pitch, but then declined. Shortly thereafter, NBC aired a show called "Stars Earn Stripes" that revolved around celebrity contestants competing in skill-based competitions based on military maneuvers. In the court's view, both shows demonstrated a similar theme and mood ("appreciation and respect for military personnel") and "uncannily similar" kinds of contestants (e.g., professional wrestlers, former *Dancing with the Stars* competitors). Unlike in the case of Ms. Simmons, the court concluded that when "[v]iewing the protectable aspects of the works as a whole," a reasonable trier of fact could determine the two works to be substantially similar.[29]

Arnstein identified *who* was relevant for determining copyright infringement, but the decision did not specify *what* its test for infringement was supposed to measure. A judge or jury examining two works for substantial similarity needs to know what level of similarity should

be considered "substantial." Other legal decisions supplied this information, instructing that the task for the trier of fact was to determine if
the "aesthetic appeal of the [defendant's] work is the same" as the
plaintiff's work.[30] At the same time, "aesthetic appeal" is not a term
with a clear legal or philosophical definition. Maybe two reality shows
featuring celebrities enduring military training had the same aesthetic
appeal whereas programs showcasing the personal lives of women in
hip hop did not, but it is hard to know why. Somehow the moods and
themes in the first case were insufficiently similar but not in the second.
The shared use of comparable kinds of celebrity contestants was
probative of aesthetic similarity for the military reality show, but featuring the same contestant in both hip-hop shows – Chrissy Lampkin –
was not. By tethering infringement to aesthetic experience, copyright
law makes the infringement analysis highly uncertain and often
inconsistent.

This is not to say that there are no legal guideposts for determining
a work's aesthetic appeal. Over the years, in attempting to define the
parameters of the aesthetic experience, courts made certain assumptions. Like the creative process, the audience's aesthetic experience of
the fruits of that process is considered subjective and unmeasurable,
making a quantitative analysis impossible. Any effort to empirically
determine the features of copyrighted works that audiences would pay
the most attention to or that would rank highest in their aesthetic
evaluations is doomed to fail and therefore excluded from the substantial similarity analysis. Moreover, the belief that responses to art occur
rapidly makes judges skeptical of lengthy deliberations over work
similarities. As we will see, neuroaesthetic studies challenge some of
these assumptions about the aesthetic experience, placing the foundation of substantial similarity on unstable ground.

MOVING FROM EMPIRICAL INVESTIGATION
TO UNQUANTIFIABLE INTUITION

By stressing aesthetic concerns, the substantial similarity test leaves out
other potential commonalities that could inform the infringement
analysis. One might envision a different substantial similarity test that

asked the jury in the "Stairway to Heaven" case to tally up what matches and what does not in a measure-by-measure analysis of the two musical works, perhaps with the court first screening out those aspects of Randy Wolfe's song that are not copyrightable. Or, if market harm was the *sine qua non* of infringement, Tashera Simmons' case might have hinged on an assessment of whether VH1's "Love & Hip Hop" empire hurt the potential market for "Hip Hop Wives." The substantial similarity test rejects either approach, prohibiting direct consideration of perceived similarities or financial harm, instead resting infringement on the unknowable aesthetic sensibilities of the trier of fact.

The critical precedent that eventually led to aesthetic appeal becoming the *sine qua non* of infringement was *Daly* v. *Palmer*. That case, decided seventy-five years before *Arnstein*, signaled a move from defining infringement as bodily appropriation of copyrighted expression to something broader and ineffable. Beginning with *Daly*, in the mid- to late-nineteenth century, "[t]he infringement analysis slowly shifted from having a strong focus on verbatim copying to encompassing increasingly remote levels of similarity."[31]

Playwright Augustin Daly wrote a melodrama with a sensationalist scene featuring a character tied to a railroad track by a villain, the character then rescued from a steaming locomotive by the play's protagonist in the nick of time. When a theatre owner staged another play with a similar railroad scene, Daly sued for copyright infringement. A federal court in New York found in Daly's favor explaining:

> it is a piracy, if the appropriated series of events, when represented on the stage, although performed by new and different characters, using different language, is recognized by the spectator, through any of the senses to which the representation is addressed, as conveying substantially the same impressions to, and exciting the same emotions in, the mind, in the same sequence or order.[32]

For decades, courts had assessed whether infringement occurred by looking to whether the actual language of the original work had been copied by the defendant. For example, Harriet Beecher Stowe failed in her infringement action against an unauthorized translator of her book *Uncle Tom's Cabin* because the German translation did not contain the exact same English words as the original. The *Daly* decision conceived of the copyright interest more broadly, not as a right in the four corners of a tangible object, but as a right to prevent others from recreating aspects of a copyrighted work in a way that would prompt the same aesthetic experience. *Daly* began to shift substantial similarity away from an empirical investigation of tangible qualities to a question that relied on unquantifiable intuition to answer.

Daly's vision of aesthetic experience did not lend itself to a rigorous picking apart of works. By locating infringement in the registering of "impressions" and "emotions," *Daly* implied that substantial similarity could not be determined on the basis of careful study, or an exacting breakdown of two works into their component parts. As one early twentieth-century court explained, because "copyright, like all statutes, is made for plain people . . . infringement must be something which ordinary observations would cause to be recognized"; if "dissection rather than observation" is needed "to discern any resemblance," then there is no infringement.[33] More recently, a federal court of appeals described the "touchstone of the [substantial similarity] analysis" as only countenancing those differences that the ordinary observer had not "set out to detect."[34]

To protect the impressionist quality of aesthetic reaction, courts largely prohibit attempts to determine substantial similarity by compiling lists of similarities and differences in the works at issue. Determining aesthetic response should not involve a "catalogue," explained Judge Learned Hand. Instead the "proper approach . . . must be more ingenious, more like that of a spectator, who would rely upon the complex of his impressions of each character."[35] Courts today describe the infringement comparison as one of "overall look and feel." Thanks to the focus on aesthetic response, "copyright infringement is supposed to be based on a gestalt reaction,"[36] not an evaluation of "minute differences between the two works."[37] The law offers two extremely broad suggestions for locating this gestalt reaction: substantial similarity should be based on the audience's pleasurable sensations and these sensations occur rapidly upon exposure to the creative works at issue.

Aesthetic Pleasure

In attempting to describe the components of aesthetic experience, courts since *Daly* have highlighted audience pleasure. Copyright decisions speak of a certain substance in creative works that is pleasurable to the senses and can be elucidated without much effort. In a formulation endorsed by several federal courts, *Arnstein* framed the substantial similarity analysis as "whether defendant took from plaintiff's works so much of what is pleasing to the ears of lay listeners ... that defendant wrongfully appropriated something which belongs to the plaintiff."[38] Courts equate that which is "pleasing" in the aesthetic experience with beauty, explaining that it is the "beautiful" aspects of a work that must be protected from appropriation by others.[39] Put another way, the trier of fact must assess what the audience would consider of value in the plaintiff's work and determine if that pleasurable essence is replicated in the defendant's work. This linking of audience pleasure and aesthetic response turns what might be a logical inquiry into the tangible material of the plaintiff's work into one that is subjective and resistant to judicial inquiry.

For copyright law, the pleasure enjoyed by audiences is inevitably subjective and intuitive. Take these comments from a court on how the trier of fact should put herself in the shoes of the average audience member. Substantial similarity, the court explained:

> is not a legal conclusion; rather it involves the audience in an interactive process with the author of the work in question, and calls on us to transfer from our inward nature a human interest and a semblance of truth sufficient to procure for those shadows of imagination that willing suspension of belief for the moment, which constitutes poetic faith.[40]

This "interactive process" between author and audience is unavoidably personal, requiring judges to abandon their penchant for objective analysis. The court went on to employ a quote from *Hamlet* to describe this process, stating that "this interactive assessment is by nature an individualized one that will provoke a varied response in each juror, 'for what makes the unskillful laugh, cannot but make the judicious grieve'."[41] In other words, the pleasure experienced by audiences cannot be derived through objective calculation. It must be subjectively experienced by the trier of fact in the way that the audience itself experienced it or would experience it.

Hence, courts rely on intuition to assess a work's aesthetic appeal rather than reasoned evaluation or guidance from experts in the field.

Instinct is what matters for measuring aesthetic response, not reasoned deliberation. Dissenting in the *Arnstein* case, Judge Clark objected that "[m]usic is a matter of the intellect as well as the emotions; that is why eminent musical scholars insist upon the employment of the intellectual faculties for a just appreciation of music."[42] Yet Judges Frank and Hand took a different path, now followed by all other federal courts, that asks for the immediate reactions of the trier of fact, unaided by scholarly expertise, to diagnose the actionable essence of creative works.

The downside to characterizing aesthetic response as inherently subjective is that it makes that response impossible to pin down, leaving copyright litigants on uncertain terrain and the trier of fact reliant on instinct to decide the ultimate issue of infringement. Courts acknowledge this demerit – years before hearing the *Led Zeppelin* case, the same court described its jurisdiction's infringement test as "a mere subjective judgment" that is "virtually devoid of analysis" – without coming up with any workable corrective.[43] Responding to criticism that its test for substantial similarity was too vague, the same court of appeals that decided *Arnstein* somewhat feebly responded that the trier of fact must "identify precisely the particular aesthetic decisions – original to the plaintiff and copied by the defendant – *that might be thought* to make the designs similar in the aggregate."[44] Yet the court offered no guidance for determining how to make this precise identification of what the audience might think similar. Outsiders cannot help with this identification. Because aesthetic judgment is an intuitive process not a deliberative one, the trier of fact must rely on her sensibilities alone and "detect piracy *without any aid or suggestions or critical analysis by others.*"[45]

Time

Another component of aesthetic appeal involves its temporal scope. Courts have suggested a time limit for judges and juries attempting to discern the aesthetic response of ordinary observers and listeners. The probable response by the ordinary observer after labored scrutiny of the works at issue is not what the analysis asks for. Instead, the analysis asks for only the "spontaneous and immediate" experience of audiences.[46] The "visceral reactions" of the observer are what determine infringement.[47] Courts sometimes refer to the "ordinary observer" as the "casual observer," implying that a speedy, non-deliberative processing of the works at issue is the appropriate means for calculating substantial similarity.[48]

As a result, rapid responses to creative works have more validity for the infringement analysis than ones drawn out over time. Aesthetic experience should be immediate: "There is a notion that juries ought to be able to look at works and experience a gut reaction."[49] Unless the work at issue is particularly complex or technical, the work is "seen to speak for itself," obviating the need for lengthy scrutiny.[50] Even comparisons that may be relatively challenging because the plaintiff's work and the defendant's work are in different media are evaluated for their instantaneous impression. For example, a court assessing whether a book and a movie were substantially similar explained that it compared the two works "to determine a lay observer's *immediate* response."[51] In this view, the rapidity of aesthetic judgment makes it more reliable in diagnosing improper copying, not less.

This call for immediate impressions rather than careful comparison vexes some opponents of the ordinary observer test. "Why should the ordinary observer be expected to detect spontaneously and immediately the theft which probably took weeks and months to disguise?" queried one exasperated law professor.[52] The answer is that substantial similarity investigates aesthetic encounters, which courts believe to be instantaneous phenomena. Many other areas of the law require the trier of fact to intuit the behavior of outsiders. Tort law famously asks whether the defendant's conduct matches the conduct of the "reasonable person." Yet, because copyright law asks the trier of fact to intuit the reasonable person's *aesthetic* response, courts stress that there is no time for the reasonable person to engage in lengthy deliberation or analysis.

THE SCIENCE OF HOW AESTHETIC DECISIONS ARE MADE

Even as courts insist that aesthetic judgment is impossible to measure, neuroscientists are becoming more and more adept at quantifying its different components. As neuroaesthetic studies reveal more specifics about aesthetic choice, copyright law's longstanding insistence that aesthetic choice cannot be interrogated may weaken. Researchers claim to be able to distinguish the hallmarks of aesthetic experience from functional experiences. They identify a "fundamentally different pattern of neurophysiological activation" for artwork that audience members perceive as "best in terms of aesthetic quality"[53] or "the most aesthetically moving."[54] Scientists are also becoming adept at separating aesthetic judgment into its component parts. The neural evidence of an audience's processing of an artwork's pictorial content can be distinguished from evidence of the audience's processing of the artist's style.[55] Just as neuroscience has improved our understanding of the creative process, it offers critical information on the mechanics of aesthetic judgment of the fruits of that process.

Neuroscientific study of human reactions to music provides a good example of how brain science can contribute to our understanding of aesthetic encounters. "Aesthetic listening" experiments purport to offer a "traceable" mental process for the perception, understanding, and enjoyment of musical events.[56] These experiments reveal the significance of particular portions of musical works to the listener. Tell-tale neural signals distinguish sounds serving as a real stimulus that can contribute to the aesthetic experience from sounds that the listener will only experience as noise.[57]

Perhaps most relevant to the substantial similarity calculation, neuroaesthetics investigates which aspects of artistic work are most salient to audiences. Understandably, infringement doctrine asks the trier of fact to render a judgment as to aesthetic salience. For example, when an R&B songwriter accused Usher and Justin Bieber of wrongfully appropriating his musical work, an appellate court reversed a substantial similarity determination in the defendants' favor. It faulted the trial court for ignoring the importance of the choruses to both songs and applying a "purely quantitative inquiry" to the question of "aesthetic appeal." Because choruses are the part of a song "that many listeners will recognize immediately or hear in their minds when a song title is mentioned," the court considered chorus similarities "disproportionately significant."[58]

This makes sense. If one is concerned with protecting the creative incentives of authors, it is appropriate to use copyright law to protect the original aspects of a work that are most noticeable or important to audiences. The problem is that the court of appeal in the Justin Bieber case relied on a hunch about audience reaction to the songs' choruses, not any objective information about how the choruses were actually perceived. In the past, this kind of information about aesthetic salience was largely unknowable so hunches were all judges could go on. Today, imaging technologies offer a data-driven and finer-grained portrait of aesthetic choice.

Finding Beauty

Aesthetic salience can be diagnosed in a variety of ways. Neuroaesthetic researchers often equate such salience with pleasure. As the cognitive psychologist Steven Pinker writes, art's primary function is to "press our pleasure buttons."[59] Pleasure facilitates the brain's attentional networks as pleasurable sensations prompt a reallocation of cognitive resources for enhanced processing of a stimulus.

A related subject of neuroaesthetic research is how audiences recognize beauty – a logical avenue of inquiry given beauty's role in the popular imagination as the primary criterion for making aesthetic judgments. One might question the ability to interrogate something seemingly as amorphous as beauty. We have all heard the saying that beauty is in the eye of the beholder. But scientists searching for the biological signs of perceived beauty contend that "the neural activity seems to be detectable and quantifiable, which makes it apt for empirical investigation."[60] Cultural differences exist, but there is also a shared, unconscious sense of what is attractive.[61]

Some work finds that the experience of beauty has its own unique neural signature. Scientists have identified "a single faculty of beauty into which different senses feed."[62] When audience members are asked to rate stimuli as either "ugly," "indifferent," or "beautiful," the stimuli designated as "beautiful" generate particular brain behaviors. Multiple experiments correlate the experience of beauty with activity in a particular area of the brain: the medial orbitofrontal cortex or mOFC.[63] Other studies demonstrate links between patterns of neural activity across the brain and the experiences of aesthetic contemplation and pleasure.[64]

It is not just that brain-imaging tools offer a clue as to when an observer or listener will consider something to be beautiful. Neuroaesthicians are more ambitious, leveraging their current understandings to develop ways to calculate the strength of an aesthetic response. In one highly publicized study, participants listened to unfamiliar fragments of music and were allocated a fixed sum that they used to "vote" on which fragments they would like to listen to again. The degree of neural activity in particular brain regions predicted the amount of money participants were willing to pay to listen to their preferred fragments a second or third time. The activated brain regions had been ascertained from previous research to be integral to "emotional processing and value-guided decision-making." Copyright law assumes that our intuitive reactions to art cannot be measured, but, according to the study's authors, their findings reveal "a mechanism for valuation of stimuli of abstract importance."[65] Neuroscientists envision a future where they can calculate the depth of an audience's aesthetic reactions. As two leaders in the field contend, "the subjective experience of beauty and of ugliness can be objectively ascertained and measured" and will "take aesthetics very much into the subjective, though quantifiable, arena."[66]

Admittedly, there is more to aesthetic processing than experiencing beauty and pleasure. Both cognitive psychologists and philosophers agree that dislike, disgust, and other aesthetic emotions are important as well. But the subjective experience of beauty is directly linked to the sensation of pleasure, something that is assuredly at the heart of aesthetic judgment. In general, there is a significant overlap between the hedonic basic pleasures we experience through activities like sex and eating and the higher-order pleasures we associate with aesthetic experience. Consciously or not, we find these experiences rewarding and fMRI and EEG technologies have the ability to reveal when the mind's reward center has been activated from such experiences.

As noted, in seeming agreement with neuroaesthetic research, courts articulating the test for substantial similarity speak of "beauty" and "pleasure," encouraging the trier of fact to examine their subjective experience of the works at issue for those qualities and feelings. Those same courts may be unwilling, however, to equate aesthetic reward with the reward from stroking a romantic partner's hair or eating a mouth-watering cheeseburger. Fortunately, neuroscience offers the potential for separating the sensory rewards of art from other experiences. As literary scholar Gabrielle Starr writes in her investigation of the aesthetic experience of beauty, "the finding that reward activations for painting straddles both the dorsal and ventral regions of the striatum begins to support the possibility ... that aesthetic rewards may be processed differently."[67] Starr goes on to note that research shows not only a particularity in how aesthetic rewards are processed in the brain but in how those rewards are integrated. Aesthetic experience, like other pleasurable experiences, integrates reward signals to engage emotional processes. But this engagement involves a particularly large, integrated system in the brain – the default mode network – that is not necessarily activated in response to other sensory rewards. The default mode network is associated with introspection and self-assessment, making it a likely locus of activity for aesthetic judgment.

In a related vein, there is a measurable biological difference between the reward received from a stimulus someone "likes" and the reward received from a stimulus someone "wants."[68] It is hypothesized that liking – what the neuroscientist Anjan Chatterjee describes as "pleasure without an acquisitive impulse" [69] – is what it means to experience aesthetic pleasure. We can enjoy a painting without thinking we need to take it home. One neuroscientist contends that "the central question regarding aesthetic experience is to shed light on the difference between 'liking' and 'wanting' processes."[70] This maps onto a central component of aesthetic theory – the idea that aesthetic judgment requires disinterested appreciation, i.e., enjoying art for its own sake and not as a means for serving our own interests. If the aesthetic pleasure at issue in the infringement analysis is the pleasure from liked but not wanted rewards, then perhaps an ability to determine when the neural signature for liking has been triggered upon experiencing a particular creative work could be relevant to substantial similarity.

It is important to state here that neuroscientific measurements are not reliable or specific enough to determine the substantial similarity analysis on their own. The overlap between aesthetic pleasure and other sensory pleasures can be difficult to disentangle as is the difference between "liking" rewards and "wanting" rewards. Nevertheless, the possibility of a future where aesthetic judgment lends itself to quantification deserves serious consideration. A roadmap to the particular aspects of creative works that produce the greatest devotion of attentional resources and prompt the most pleasurable sensations in their audiences would seem to be just what the substantial similarity analysis cries out for. Some tangible evidence of aesthetic response, even if incomplete, might be better than copyright law's current failure to try to understand audiences. Instead of guessing at the importance of a particular musical passage, the trier of fact could be provided with neural proof of that passage's salience. Admittedly, at this point, neuroscience can only offer a very partial picture of aesthetic reaction; it would serve as a supplement to, not a substitute for, the current substantial similarity inquiry. As the author of one copyright treatise writes regarding the use of psychological research more broadly, "[t]hese inquiries would not supplant the ordinary observer test, but instead assist in understanding how much weight the ordinary observer should give to similarities and differences."[71]

Most importantly, even if brain imaging is unlikely in the short term to be accepted as evidence in individual copyright cases, neuroaesthetic research will force courts to abandon the current assumption that any objective analysis of aesthetic response is impossible. Copyright law operates under the belief that our aesthetic experiences cannot be measured. As a result, substantial similarity decisions are not specified by the trier of fact or interrogated by courts in review. This, in turn, makes it extremely difficult to dispose of the issue of substantial similarity before trial. Copyright law exhorts triers of fact to examine their experiences of "beauty" and "pleasure" in deciding infringement claims yet offers little to no guidance for what those legally relevant sensory categories should mean. Even if neuroaesthetics cannot yet fully break down our experiences of aesthetic pleasure and beauty, it calls into question copyright law's refusal to countenance any objective analysis of how we respond to creative works.

Immediacy

As discussed, copyright law assumes that aesthetic judgment is both rapid and stable. This assumption has consequences for the copyright infringement analysis. It is the lay observer's "immediate response" and "spontaneous reaction" that is relevant to identifying the protect-able essence of the copyrighted work. Any longer appreciation of the work is considered illegitimate, either because courts assume that any later evaluation of the work will not alter the original judgment or because the audience's instant experience is deemed a better proxy for the market behavior of interested patrons. Dissection of an artistic work into its component parts is discouraged because such an analyt-ical approach seems unlikely to improve outcomes if the goal is to recreate the actual speed at which audiences evaluate creative expression.

Neuroscientists investigate the temporal dynamics of aesthetic judgment, something that has only been guessed at by the federal courts. Their research has coalesced around a two-phase description of the timing involved in aesthetic appreciation. First, there is an initial implicit processing phase that captures "low-level" features of the perceived object. Second, there is a higher-level processing phase involving "a deeper aesthetic evaluation."[72]

The critical thing to note here is that both phases take place rapidly. The first low-level phase occurs 300–400 milliseconds after presenta-tion of a stimulus. The second phase takes place almost immediately thereafter, just a few hundred milliseconds after stimulus presentation. Much happens in this short time frame. An observer's brain can process the content in an artwork in 10 milliseconds and the artwork's style in 50 milliseconds.[73]

This research shows that aesthetic judgment occurs instantan-eously, in a similar fashion to the "spontaneous reaction" described by the courts. Strong preferences form in this short window as the brain conducts both sensory and semantic analyses of the stimulus at issue. Judgment of a creative work's beauty occurs in a split second.[74]

Our aesthetic judgments are not just rapid, but reliable. Within 750 milliseconds, listeners can judge how much they like a musical excerpt and do so with a high degree of accuracy, i.e., the judgment about that excerpt remains the same even after hearing the entire piece.[75] One might think that past experiences with both similar and different cre-ative works, as well as other relevant memories, would be determinative in this process. Yet research reveals that we do not need to comb through our frames of reference to enjoy art. In contrast to the process of generating creative works, "aesthetic pleasure comes into being without analysis, consideration, or reliance on – or reference to – former perceptual experiences."[76] Our previous experiences are relevant to aesthetic appreciation but they are not necessary.

Discerning the speed at which aesthetic judgments occur is important because the faster these judgments, the more one can argue that there is little time in this process for deliberately weighing a work's different components. One cognitive scientist puts it this way: "Since the timescale of the brain's functional activity is in the order of milliseconds, complex processes take place very quickly, leading to a qualitative, simple subjective conclusion about the beauty of a stimulus."[77] In fact, exposing jurors to the same expressive materials too often or for too long a period of time can produce habituation and "aesthetic fatigue," potentially changing their perception of the materials as compared to the ordinary observer.[78] Hence, neuroaesthetic research offers evidentiary support for the substantial similarity status quo when it comes to the timing of aesthetic reactions in the courtroom. Casual, fast reviews of stimuli provide the best window into the aesthetic experience. Lengthy deliberations over the merits of a creative work can distort or partially obscure those merits.

RESPONDING TO NEUROAESTHETIC SKEPTICS

Neuroaesthetics is not without its skeptics. Some worry that, despite advances in spatial resolution and processing speed, imaging technologies cannot hope to describe a cognitive process as complex as aesthetic judgment. Others contend that neuroscience offers nothing to the study of aesthetics because it posits biological causation for a process that is much more ethereal. Finally, there is a concern that neuroaesthetic research fails to capture the real-world context of artistic appreciation.

It is true that the process of aesthetic judgment is complex. Even though it occurs incredibly quickly, aesthetic judgment relies on a host of mental processes – perception, cognition, and affect – in a dynamic process. Critics who complain that aesthetic judgment cannot be located in one area of the brain are right. Researchers cannot examine a single biological unit to determine when someone is processing artistic stimuli nor can judges study one neural terrain to determine if an audience will recognize one creative work as coming from another. Moreover, because many of the neural processes behind aesthetic response also apply to other sensory experiences, researchers need to be careful to avoid the problem of reverse inference. It is useful to discover that engaging in a particular cognitive process – like a judgment that a creative work is "beautiful" – produces activity in particular brain regions. But it is not fair to infer that activity in a particular brain region always signals that the subject is engaging in a particular cognitive process.

Yet just because the neural circuitry of aesthetic response is complex that does not mean that it is unknowable or that we cannot hope to understand it better. Scientists realize that they need to study neural networks acting across the brain at different times and not just the activity of a single region. At this point, neuroscientists are not looking for an "art button" in the brain. Instead, they apply advanced cognitive models that involve multiple brain regions and overlapping neural networks. As noted, particular attention has been paid to the default mode network, a neural circuit that constantly measures the sensory environment and, hence, appears germane to the processing of artistic stimuli. Other networks track the reward value of a stimulus, which can be useful in determining what is pleasing to the eye or ear of an audience member.[79] The problem of reverse inference is a concern, but it requires caution before attributing neural activity solely to an aspect of the aesthetic experience, not a wholesale abandonment of neuroaesthetic research.

Skeptics might press their point by maintaining that even if researchers acknowledge the biological complexity of the aesthetic experience, that complexity represents a barrier to understanding audiences that researchers have yet to cross. Scientists have gotten better in the last decade at decoding the different brain regions involved in aesthetic encounters, but they are still far removed from answering some of the basic questions one might want to know to fully comprehend the physiology of audience reaction. For example, at this point, when someone recognizes a particular stimulus, brain scans cannot determine whether the person is relying on a true memory (i.e., something that really happened to the person) instead of a false one. The philosopher John Hyman questioned what good can come of neuroaesthetic study if we cannot tell if an audience member viewing an image of a voluptuous woman is responding to the artistry used to create the image or sensuous impulses one might feel regardless of creative technique.[80]

Hyman is right that neuroscientists have not cracked the code on exactly what makes aesthetic experiences unique. But they are aware of this. Experimenters routinely caution that aesthetic responses overlap with other biological processes and that reactions to creative works can mimic reactions to other stimuli. Aesthetic experiences involve many of the same biological processes as other experiences but this does not make their study useless. As it stands now, the substantial similarity test offers no predictive ability for litigants or content for courts in review. Insights into how audiences process creative works (and confirmation that there is indeed a unique biology to aesthetic thought) represent an improvement from the status quo even if it is not yet possible to identify every part of what makes aesthetic responses unique.

Hyman's critique also seems to fault neuroscientists for not offering an answer to a question that has haunted aesthetic philosophers for centuries. He rightly contends that fMRI imaging cannot tell us what should be considered art and what should not. But it is not necessary for neuroscience to resolve this philosophical conundrum before it can help understand the aesthetic experience. Brain scans will never be able to explain what makes for good artwork.

Instead, neuroaesthetics can provide information on the biological mechanisms behind the enjoyment of some artworks but not others. If one defines aesthetics to include the study of all stimuli generating positive emotions, then it would seem that neuroscientists can provide valuable information on aesthetic responses. This may not match Hyman's definition of aesthetics, but that is not the fault of scientists trying to describe a mental process while avoiding making normative claims about art appreciation.

Other objections to neuroaesthetic study are more specific. One might question the ability of neuroscientists to recreate the real-world conditions of aesthetic judgment. This is important because the substantial similarity test calls for the trier of fact to experience creative works in the same manner as their intended audiences. Seeing an image of a painting while being scanned in an fMRI machine is not the same as seeing the original in a museum. Past experiments often confronted participants with long successions of artworks divorced from their typical context.

Those working in neuroaesthetics are sensitive to these concerns. Contexts have been varied in an effort to determine when a contextual change will influence the neural processes behind aesthetic judgment. For example, researchers try to partially recreate the art museum context by telling some subjects that the images they are viewing are "gallery art." And not all studies are undertaken in artificial lab conditions. Researchers have sampled the reactions of actual museum visitors and live concert goers. Moreover, as the technology for neural imaging becomes more portable, the opportunities for recreating the context surrounding creative works will only multiply. Already, in private industry and in government studies, researchers use portable EEG devices to measure subjects' neural responses in grocery stores and on battlefields. Current technologies do not allow for an inquiry into all aspects of aesthetic encounters, but the ability to assess audience reaction when experiencing a creative work represents a marked improvement over the black box that currently houses the substantial similarity analysis.

Notes

1. Skidmore v. Led Zeppelin, 905 F.3d 1116, 1125 (9th Cir. 2018).
2. *Id.*
3. Curwood v. Affiliated Distributors, Inc., 283 F. 223, 228 (S.D.N.Y. 1922).
4. Sheldon v. Metro-Goldwyn Pictures Corp., 7 F. Supp. 837, 842 (S.D.N.Y. 1934).
5. Sheldon v. Metro-Goldwyn Pictures Corp., 81 F.2d 49, 56 (2d Cir. 1936).
6. Shyamkrisha Balganesh, *The Questionable Origins of the Copyright Infringement Analysis*, 69 STAN. L. REV. 791, 801 (2016).
7. Arnstein v. Porter, 154 F.2d 464, 467 (2d Cir. 1946).
8. *Id.* at 468.
9. Sheldon, 7 F. Supp. at 842.
10. Nutt v. Nat'l Inst., Inc. for Improvement of Memory, 31 F.2d 236, 238 (2d Cir. 1929).
11. MacDonald v. Du Maurier, 44 F.2d 696, 701 (2d Cir. 1944).

[12] Shaw v. Lindheim, 919 F.2d 1353, 1361 (9th Cir. 1990).

[13] Lyons P'ship, L.P. v. Morris Costumes, Inc., 243 F.3d 789, 801 (4th Cir. 2001).

[14] Ideal Toy Corp. v. Kenner Prods., 443 F. Supp. 291, 297 (S.D.N.Y. 1977).

[15] Warner Bros. v. American Broadcasting Cos., 720 F.2d 231 (2d Cir. 1983).

[16] IMMANUEL KANT, CRITIQUE OF JUDGMENT § 9 at 61 (Werner S. Pluhar trans. 1987).

[17] Id. § 7 at 55–56.

[18] Valentina Cazzato, *Gender Differences in the Neural Underpinning of Perceiving and Appreciating the Beauty of the Body*, 264 BEHAV. BRAIN RES. 188, 194–95 (2014); Camilo J. Cela-Conde et al., *Sex-Related Similarities and Differences in the Neural Correlates of Beauty*, 106 PROC. NAT´L ACAD. SCI. 3847, 3851 (2009).

[19] Juan Garcia-Prieto et al., *Neurocognitive Decoding of Aesthetic Appreciation, in* MULTIMODAL OSCILLATION-BASED CONNECTIVITY THEORY 87, 97 (S. Palva ed. 2016).

[20] Anjan Chatterjee & Oshin Vartanian, *Neuroscience of Aesthetics*, 1369 ANNALS OF N.Y. ACAD. SCI. 172 (2016).

[21] Ulrich Kirk et al., *Brain Correlates of Aesthetic Expertise: A Parametric fMRI Study*, 69 BRAIN & COGNITION 306, 309 (2009).

[22] Helmut Leder, *Next Steps in Neuroaesthetics: Which Processes and Processing Stages to Study?*, 7 J. PSYCH. AESTHETICS CREATIVITY & ARTS 27, 33 (2013).

[23] Edward A. Vessel et al., *Stronger Shared Taste for Natural Aesthetic Domains Than for Artifacts of Human Culture*, 179 COGNITION 121, 122 (2018).

[24] Beatriz Calvo-Merino et al., *Experts See It All: Configural Effects in Action Observation*, 74 PSYCH. RES. 400 (2010).

[25] Jon O. Lauring, *Visual Art, in* AN INTRODUCTION TO NEUROAESTHETICS 115, 125 (Jon O. Lauring ed. 2014); Cristina Rosazza et al., *Early Involvement of Dorsal and Ventral Pathways in Visual Word Recognition: An ERP Study*, 1272 BRAIN RES. 32, 32–33 (2009).

[26] Note, Isabel Corngold, *Copyright Infringement and the Science of Music Memory: Applying Cognitive Psychology to the Substantial Similarity Test*, 45 AIPLA Q.J. 319, 339–42 (2017).

[27] Garcia-Prieto et al., *supra*, at 98.

[28] 8th Wonder Entmt. v. Viacom Intl., 2016 WL 6882832, at *7–*8 (C.D. Cal., Nov. 22, 2015).

[29] Dillon v. NBCUniversal Media, 2013 WL 3581938, at *7 (C.D. Cal., June 18, 2013).

[30] Peter Pan Fabrics, Inc. v. Martin Weiner Corp., 274 F.2d 487, 489 (2d Cir. 1960).

[31] Oren Bracha, *Not De Minimis*, 68 AM. U. L. REV. 139, 171 (2018).

[32] Daly v. Palmer, 6 F. Cas. 1132, 1138 (C.C.S.D.N.Y. 1868) (No. 3552).

[33] Dymov v. Bolton, 11 F.2d 690, 692 (2d Cir. 1926).

[34] Sturdza v. United Arab Emirates, 281 F.3d 1287, 1296 (D.C. Cir. 2002).

[35] Nichols v. Universal Pictures Corp. 45 F.2d 119, 123 (2d Cir. 1930).

[36] Rebecca Tushnet, *Worth a Thousand Words: The Images of Copyright*, 125 HARV. L. REV. 683, 736 (2012).

[37] Atari, Inc. v. North Am. Philips Consumer Electronics Corp., 672 F.2d 607, 618 (7th Cir. 1982). *See also* Copeland v. Bieber, 789 F.3d 484, 489 (4th Cir. 2015) ("[W]e analyze works as cohesive wholes, without distinguishing between protected and unprotected elements, just as the works' intended audiences likely would encounter them in the marketplace.").

[38] Arnstein, 154 F.2d at 473.

[39] See, for example, King Features Syndicate v. Fleischer, 299 F. 533, 534, 536 (2d Cir. 1924).

[40] Shaw, 919 F.2d at 1360.

[41] *Id.*

[42] Arnstein, 154 F.2d at 476–77 (Clark, J., dissenting).

[43] Shaw, 919 F.2d at 1357–58. Substantial similarity in this jurisdiction requires satisfaction of both an "extrinsic test" and an "intrinsic test." The extrinsic test allows an analysis of similarities according to objective criteria and a filtering out of unprotectable elements. If the plaintiff satisfies the extrinsic test, the trier of fact must then evaluate infringement under the intrinsic test. As noted by the court, judges typically supply no more than a single paragraph of analysis to justify their determination under the intrinsic similarity determination. *Id.*

[44] Tufenkian Import/Export Ventures, Inc. v. Einstein Moomjy, Inc., 338 F.3d 127, 134 (2d Cir. 2003) (emphasis added).

[45] Peel & Co. v. Rug Mkt., 238 F.3d 391, 398 (5th Cir. 2001) (emphasis added).

[46] *Id.*

[47] 4 MELVILLE B. NIMMER & DAVID NIMMER, NIMMER ON COPYRIGHT 13–100.1 (2019).

[48] United Feature Syndicate, Inc. v. Koons, 817 F. Supp. 370, 377 (S.D.N.Y. 1993).

[49] Zahr K. Said, *A Transactional Theory of the Reader in Copyright Law*, 102 IOWA L. REV. 605, 639 (2017).

[50] Zahr K. Said, *Reforming Copyright Interpretation*, 28 HARV. J. L. & TECH. 469, 502 n.232 (2015).

[51] Randolph v. Dimension Films, 634 F. Supp. 2d 779, 792 (S.D. Tex. 2009) (emphasis added).

[52] Robert Fuller Fleming, *Substantial Similarity: Where the Plots Really Thicken*, 19 COPYRIGHT L. SYMP. (ASCAP) 252, 275 (1971).

[53] G. GABRIELLE STARR, FEELING BEAUTY: THE NEUROSCIENCE OF AESTHETIC EXPERIENCE 59–63 (2013).

[54] Vessel et al., *supra*, at 9.

[55] M. Dorothee Augustin et al., *The Neural Time Course of Art Perception: An ERP Study on the Processing of Style versus Content in Art*, 49 NEUROPSYCHOLOGIA 2071, 2072 (2011).

[56] Mark Reybrouck et al., *Brain Connectivity Networks and the Aesthetic Experience of Music*, 107 BRAIN SCI. 10 (2018).

[57] PAUL B. ARMSTRONG, HOW LITERATURE PLAYS WITH THE BRAIN: THE NEUROSCIENCE OF READING AND ART 14, 45 (2013).

[58] Copeland v. Bieber, 789 F.3d 484, 493–95 (4th Cir. 2015).

[59] STEVEN PINKER, HOW THE MIND WORKS 524–25 (1997).

[60] Reybrouck et al., *supra*, at 3.

[61] THOMAS HILGERS, AESTHETIC DISINTERESTEDNESS: ART, EXPERIENCE, AND THE SELF 17 (2017); ERIC R. KANDEL, THE AGE OF INSIGHT 379 (2012).

[62] Tomohiro Ishizu & Semir Zeki, *Toward a Brain-Based Theory of Beauty*, 6 PLOS ONE 1, 1 (2011).

[63] Interestingly, activity in the OFC (orbitofrontal cortex) increased when participants were told that visual stimuli were originals you might see in a museum instead of copies. Mengfei Huang, *Human Cortical Activity Evoked by Assignment of Authenticity When Viewing Works of Art*, 5 FRONTIERS HUM. NEUROSCI. 1, 5–6 (2011).

[64] Robin Wilkins et al., *Network Science and the Effects of Music Preference on Functional Brain Connectivity: From Beethoven to Eminem*, 4 SCI. REP. 6130, at 4 (2014).

[65] Valorie N. Salimpoor et al., *Interactions between the Nucleus Accumbens and Auditory Cortices Predict Music Reward Value*, 340 SCIENCE 216, 218 (2013).

[66] Ishizu & Zeki, *supra*, at 8–9.

[67] STARR, *supra*, at 51–56.

[68] Kent C. Berridge et al., *Dissecting Components of Reward: "Liking," "Wanting," and Learning*, 9 CURRENT OP. PHARMACOLOGY 65, 65–68 (2009); Louise P. Kirsch et al., *Shaping and Reshaping the Aesthetic Brain: Emerging Perspectives on the Neurobiology of Embodied Aesthetics*, 62 NEUROSCIENCE & BIOBEHAVIORAL REV. 56, 65 (2016).

[69] ANJAN CHATTERJEE, THE AESTHETIC BRAIN, at xx (2014).

[70] Garcia-Prieto et al., *supra*, at 94.

[71] 3 WILLIAM F. PATRY, PATRY ON COPYRIGHT § 9:85 (2021).

[72] Garcia-Prieto et al., *supra*, at 95.

[73] Helmut Leder & Marcos Nadal, *Ten Years of a Model of Aesthetic Appreciation and Aesthetic Judgments: The Aesthetic Episode—Developments and Challenges in Empirical Aesthetics*, 105 BRIT. J. PSYCH. 443, 448 (2014); Eugen B. Petcu, *The Rationale for a Redefinition of Visual Art Based on Neuroaesthetic Principles*, 51 LEONARDO 59, 59 (2018).

[74] Camilo J. Cela-Conde, *The Neural Foundations of Aesthetic Appreciation*, 94 PROGRESS NEUROBIOL. 39, 42 (2011).

[75] Amy M. Belfi et al., *Rapid Timing of Musical Aesthetic Judgments*, 147 J. EXP. PSYCH: GENERAL 1531, 1532–35 (2018).

[76] Zhihong Li et al., *Aesthetic Cognitive Module Theory: A Core Structure*, 52 J. AESTHETIC EDUC. 71, 79 (2018).

[77] Cela-Conde, *supra*, at 42.

[78] STARR, *supra*, at 102; Zhihao Zhang et al., *Toward a Neuroscientifically Informed "Reasonable Person" Test* 2–3, https://papers.ssrn.com/sol3/papers .cfm?abstract_id=3876774.

[79] Steven Brown et al., *Naturalizing Aesthetics: Brain Areas for Aesthetic Appraisal Across Sensory Modalities*, 58 NEUROIMAGE 250, 255 (2011).

[80] John Hyman, *Art & Neuroscience*, *in* BEYOND MIMESIS AND CONVENTION: REPRESENTATION IN ART AND SCIENCE 245, 250 (Roman Frigg & Matthew Hunter eds., 2010).

4 SEEING DESIGN

Design patents are justified as necessary to incentivize the production of articles of aesthetic merit, but there is little legal guidance as to what makes a design aesthetically meritorious. As with copyrightable works, some judicial language indicates that meritorious designs must be creative. An older strand of design patent law ties merit to a different quality: aesthetic pleasure.[1] Both qualities – designer innovation and audience pleasure – have proven difficult to define. As described in Chapter 2, courts avoid any rigorous inquiry into the creative process for design, policing only for nearly exact matches with previous designs and nothing more. Inquiries into audience pleasure fare no better. As with copyright law's investigation of aesthetic response, design patent law reveals that judges are anxious over their ability to discern what makes a design pleasurable for consumers.[2] In fact, design patent law has largely abandoned such investigations in favor of a minimalist approach that leaves it to the marketplace, not the courts, to select the most aesthetically favorable designs. Moreover, rather than probing whether design innovation and aesthetic pleasure are at cross-purposes, design patent law blithely assumes the two qualities are complementary, i.e., that consumers naturally appreciate innovative designs.

But if courts themselves refuse to probe the links (or lack thereof) between design innovation and aesthetic judgment, others are not so bashful. Once again, neuroaesthetic research reveals specific content for evaluating a psychological phenomenon the courts have long assumed cannot be interrogated by outsiders. A vast amount of academic and applied research investigates what makes for pleasing design. This research shows that we consider designs pleasing if they fall into a zone labeled the "aesthetic middle." Aesthetic preference is strongly tied to the ease with which an observer can mentally process a particular design. Although a limited amount of inventiveness may be needed to gain the observer's attention, consumers insist on simplicity, familiarity, and congruence with the relevant product category in designs – all qualities making an object easier for observers to comprehend.

This means that the two criteria for legally meritorious design – innovation and aesthetic pleasure – are in conflict. Instead of correlating with what an audience considers pleasing, innovation in design, after reaching an optimal level, quickly begins to trigger aesthetic distaste as mental processing of the design becomes more challenging. Reforming design patent law's overly permissive nonobviousness test will require judges and legislators to grapple with which criterion they consider more important.

THE NEUROSCIENCE OF DESIGN PREFERENCE

Neuroscience is particularly well-suited to interrogate the mechanics of the aesthetic appreciation of design. Visual processing is arguably the best understood mental process in modern neuroscience. "[T]here is broad consensus on the neuroanatomical substrates of different visual processes, as well as tools allowing researchers to infer mental states from neural data without needing to resort to self-report."[3] Functional magnetic resonance imaging allows researchers to determine what someone is imagining, a capability that highlights the central importance of visual mental imagery in aesthetic episodes. Researchers can now look to tell-tale signs in the brain to untangle different areas of visual aesthetic evaluation. For example, a person's processing of an artist's style is neurally different from her processing of the artwork's visual content.[4]

As discussed in Chapter 3, one might be skeptical of the ability to quantify the perception of a stimulus as "beautiful" or "pleasing." Yet scientists can pinpoint specific neural activity that reveals when we consider something attractive. As discussed earlier, several experiments link the experience of beauty with activity in the brain's medial orbitofrontal cortex or mOFC.[5] Various studies purport to quantify the strength of such responses.[6]

Moreover, consumer experience with design represents a particularly rich vein of neuroaesthetic study. Thanks to motivated private actors, there is more data on the biomechanics of our perception of commercial design than other matters of aesthetic judgment. For market researchers, it is the aesthetic responses of audiences that are of interest, not the creative processes of designers. Businesses have become more precise in their identification of the correlates of successful visual presentation. For example, brain imaging purports to distinguish designs perceived as "cool" – a very desirable consumer sentiment – from those that are just humorous.[7] Other experiments map out the biological hallmarks of image strength and vividness.[8] In sum, much more is understood about the neuroscience of design preference than in the past.

PREFERENCE AND PROCESSING FLUENCY

For our purposes, the most important finding from these neuroaesthetic investigations is the confirmation and explication of a theory of aesthetic preference labeled "the aesthetic middle." Studies reveal a consistent phenomenon when it comes to design preference: we approve of designs that deviate from the expected or status quo, but only moderately. The result is an inverted U: a design's novelty or complexity can enhance our aesthetic enjoyment, but only up to an optimal point of nonobviousness. Once that point is reached, the level of preference begins to decrease. As illustrated in Figure 4.1, we prefer the aesthetic middle: the range of designs comprised not of the avant-garde or the tried and true, but something in between.

The preference for aesthetic middle designs is remarkably durable. It translates to diverse populations, holds up among varying measures of behavioral intentions, and can be found across various forms of industrial design. In general, there is more agreement as to design aesthetics than popularly assumed. The dominance of aesthetic middle designs continues even when researchers vary subjects' background experience with relevant designs.[9]

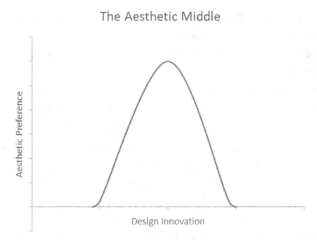

Figure 4.1 Chart representing the aesthetic middle.

Discussion of the aesthetic middle has been percolating among psychologists and market researchers for years, but neuroscience now reveals flaws in previous explanations of the phenomenon. For decades, researchers theorized that aesthetic preference was tied to mere arousal. According to this theory, the more arousing a stimulus, the more a person will prefer that stimulus, at least until a critical level is reached. Once the critical level of arousal is reached, an aversion system kicks in that becomes increasingly dominant. But psychologists found fault with this reliance on arousal to explain the aesthetic middle, pointing to studies showing aesthetic enjoyment of low-arousal stimuli. Neuroscience has supplanted the arousal theory by uncovering and studying the "reward system" in the brain that determines preference.[10]

Instead of aesthetic preference simply being dependent on arousal, it seems that our preferences are formed in a more complex manner. Research now shows that aesthetic preference is tied to the fit between the cognitive resources made available by the observer to process a given design and the resources actually required to process that design. Processing fluency is key. For example, an elaborate design will require more resources for processing. At some point, the design will demand more from the consumer than she is willing to give, resulting in a resource mismatch that leads to dissatisfaction with the design.

A winning design must gain our attention, but not in a way that overtaxes our cognitive resources. Processing fluency theory "has established itself as the single most influential explanation of aesthetic appreciation."[11]

Fluency boosts the perception of beauty and other perceptual qualities central to aesthetic preference. "The more fluently the perceiver can process an object, the more positive is his or her aesthetic response."[12] Processing fluency provides hedonic rewards. It "feels" better when we do not find the effort to perceive a design as overtaxing. Studies show that fluently processed products are liked more and judged as more beautiful.[13] Conversely, a mismatch between the cognitive resources we bring to bear in analyzing a design and the cognitive resources necessary to process that design produces feelings of distress and correspondingly low aesthetic rankings.

Psychologists began to demonstrate the role of processing fluency in forming aesthetic preference through experiments that recorded the electrical activity of facial muscle tissue upon presentations of different stimuli. High fluency was associated with stronger activity in the facial muscles indicative of positive affect. These physiological responses occurred before participants had a chance to render an overt judgment of the stimulus. Neuroscientific studies confirmed these results, detecting decreased activity in a part of the brain – the posterior occipital cortex – also indicative of positive affect when steps are taken to make visual processing more fluent.[14]

A key feature of the role of processing fluency in aesthetic preference, and one that could not be diagnosed through the reports of observers themselves, is its hidden nature. Subconscious influences steer aesthetic preference. Even very weak memories of a design – so weak that we may not realize they are being recalled – fuel more positive aesthetic evaluation.[15] Strong and stable aesthetic preferences form so rapidly – within 600 milliseconds of exposure – that they occur without our knowledge.[16] In general, the experience of processing fluency is outside of our awareness at the "fringe of consciousness."[17]

Just the subjective feeling of visual processing fluency, even if that feeling is not accurate, increases aesthetic preference. In an ingenious experiment, researchers showed study participants various images while participants simultaneously received feedback on their skin conductance response. Participants were told that high skin conductance readings meant ease of mental processing while low skin conductance readings translated to processing difficulty. In reality, the conductance feedback was randomized and had nothing to do with actual processing fluency. The more participants were made to feel that they were processing an image easily, the higher they rated the image.[18] Indeed, research shows that subjectively felt fluency has an even greater influence on aesthetic preference than objective measures of ease of visual processing and that this influence is stronger when its source is unrecognized by the observer.[19]

Some might resist this account of aesthetic preference's dependence on processing fluency by invoking examples of fine art that exhibited challenging or disruptive aesthetic qualities. The disturbing images in Picasso's *Guernica* may not trigger immediate pleasure even though the painting is recognized as a masterpiece. With such an example in mind, some psychologists and philosophers propose a dual account of aesthetic preference. In the first stage, immediate automatic processing assesses fluency which is translated into pleasure. In a second stage, instead of operating automatically, the perceiver considers her own interest, which is employed to moderate sensations of disfluency. In this later stage, it is theorized, observers can consciously act to rationalize cognitive difficulty and thereby increase their enjoyment of challenging stimuli.[20]

The dual account model is only a theory. Even if it is accurate, it likely only applies to the particulars of fine art appreciation. "Perceiving art may constitute a very special situation, that deviates in important aspects from that of every-day situations."[21] Unlike a work of fine art, design patents must be tied to some sort of product – an "article of manufacture" – and cannot be merely a design in the abstract.[22] Unlike the Picasso hanging on the wall of a museum, designs that are part of consumer goods are meant to fulfill immediate utilitarian goals and therefore trigger different expectations and correspondingly different levels of cognitive effort.[23] In other words, for the visual stimuli that are the subject of design patents, observers are more likely to lack patience for difficult-to-process visual features, penalizing such features in their aesthetic rankings.

KEY CHARACTERISTICS OF THE AESTHETIC MIDDLE

A significant problem with earlier research on the relationship between processing fluency and aesthetic judgment was that it was difficult for researchers to isolate the effects of one type of processing fluency from another. Aesthetic preference might be bolstered by a design's simplicity but it could also be shaped by the observer's familiarity with that design. There was also the question of whether familiarity improved feelings of fluency because of prior experience with the design or because of familiarity with the general category that a design falls under. For example, someone who enjoys the look of a Mini Cooper automobile may feel a subjective sense of processing fluency from prior exposure on the roads to that particular car model, various Mini Cooper models, or other examples of small "bubble cars" like the Volkswagen Beetle.

Neuroscience has helped psychologists begin to untangle these different strands of processing fluency, and thereby learn more about the aesthetic middle. *Perceptual fluency* influences aesthetic preference even without any recognition or memory of the stimulus, as with an image that is particularly visually clear or possesses sharp lines of contrast. *Repetition fluency* refers to how many prior exposures an observer has already had to a particular stimulus before rendering an aesthetic judgment. *Conceptual fluency* describes the degree to which a stimulus triggers the appropriate product category in someone's mind. A toy bank that appears like a miniature savings and loan has high conceptual fluency; a chair designed to look like a high-heeled shoe has low conceptual fluency. Each fluency type has its own unique electrical signature in the brain.[24] Researchers identify three principal dyads – simplicity/complexity, familiarity/novelty, and fit/incongruity – that roughly map on to the three fluency types. Greater insight into these different kinds of processing fluency allows for further specificity in describing the formation and function of the aesthetic middle.

Simplicity/Complexity

People prefer stimuli of moderate complexity, i.e., those designs that do not overly tax the perceptual fluency of onlookers. Stimuli that are too complex receive lower aesthetic evaluations. Complexity can be assessed in various ways and includes a variety of factors, but one way to think of visual complexity is as a measure of the amount of information a stimulus contains. Designs with greater numbers of elements or more kinds of elements are rated more complex than others.

At the same time, other design aspects operate to make a design easier to process for onlookers. The more symmetrical a design, the more the design depicts commonly experienced objects, or the more a design repeats its own elements, the easier it is for observers to process the design, resulting in less need for cognitive resources. High contrast in a design also adds to its simplicity, increasing perceptual fluency and, as a result, aesthetic preference.[25] One study of industrial design revealed that an ability to discern recognizable patterns significantly boosts aesthetic favorability ratings.[26]

All in all, designers need to tread a careful middle ground. A successful design must be visually arresting enough to capture attention as shoppers may simply pass over featureless designs. Yet the design must not be so complex that it reduces perceptual fluency to the point of aesthetic dissatisfaction. Products that tend to be thought of as design classics, like the Horwitt watch shown in Figure 4.2, employ very few elements and use readily processed vertical and horizontal orientations of those elements to create a feeling of perceptual fluency.[27]

Familiarity/Novelty

Another processing fluency variable at work in the aesthetic middle is familiarity. Measurements of blood flow and oxygenation in the brain offer ways to distinguish the role of familiarity from the role of novelty in forming aesthetic preference. Neural activity can reveal when someone is experiencing a reaction of surprise in response to a stimulus. In fact, there are even specific "novelty neurons" as well as "familiarity neurons" identified by researchers.[28]

The research shows that aesthetic preference increases (to a point) as the design becomes more prototypical, which is really a function of its familiarity to the viewer. People tend to enjoy what matches their existing knowledge base. Studies on facial attractiveness confirm a

Figure 4.2 Nathan George Horwitt "Museum" watch, ca. 1955.

strong aesthetic preference for average-looking faces as opposed to less prototypical ones.[29] Our visual processing of product design is similar, with measures of high visual typicality correlating with measures of high aesthetic preference. For example, when car designs are altered to feature greater or lesser typicality, audience aesthetic preference changes accordingly. In Figure 4.3, the car design on the left was more reflective of typical cars in the midsize category than the car on the right. Research subjects preferred the design on the left.[30]

It is also true that novel things capture our attention more successfully than familiar things. The most pleasing designs are ones that offer an optimal combination of both familiarity and novelty, rather than completely excluding one variable in favor of the other. Some designers label this the MAYA, or most advanced, yet acceptable, principle, referring to those designs that best balance repetition with novelty.

Figure 4.3 Car designs adjusted to different degrees of typicality.
Reprinted from Jan R. Landwehr et al., *Product Design for the Long Run: Consumer Responses to Typical and Atypical Designs at Different Stages of Exposure*, 77 J. Mktg. 92 (2013).

The principle explains why we scoff at seemingly outrageous costumes introduced on high fashion catwalks and offers a reason for why revisions that only slightly deviate from prior clothing designs can be so popular. Most successful industrial design tries to reach just the right amount of departure from what we have already seen and nothing more.

Fit/Incongruity

A final key variable is congruence. The observer assesses whether the resulting design is appropriate to the product category. The optimal design is one that has only moderate incongruity with regard to existing products in the category. A very limited amount of incongruity attracts attention and the devotion of greater cognitive resources, but without making categorization so difficult that it will frustrate the onlooker.

In other words, ease of categorization, which is a function of conceptual fluency, is critical to aesthetic preference. Pleasing design evokes the category of product the item is meant to be a part of. A design that registers too much distance from the product category may attract attention, but this attention will be wasted from the per-spective of commercial designers as consumers assign the design a negative aesthetic evaluation. In one experiment, eye-tracking technology was used to examine the gaze of prospective purchasers as they viewed images of various beer cans. Participants were then surveyed about their design preferences when it came to the cans as well as their thoughts on the suitability of each can design for the product category. Cans that featured unusual colors or names attracted significant visual attention yet were ranked low on suitability as well as overall aesthetic preference.[31] We like designs that fit our preconceived notions of what a design in that category should look like.

A good example of the relationship between conceptual fluency and the aesthetic middle is the story of the introduction of the Herman Miller Aeron chair. The designer of the chair expressly sought a design that looked different from all other office chairs. In contrast to the luxuriant padding and high backs of other premium office chairs, the Aeron "looked like the exoskeleton of a giant prehistoric insect."[32] A drawing of the chair, from Herman Miller's successful design patent application, is shown in Figure 4.4.[33] Even though the chair was

Figure 4.4 Herman Miller Aeron chair, US Patent No. D486,657S (Feb. 17, 2004).

engineered to be ergonomically superior to its predecessors, those who tried it awarded it low marks for comfort. Even after people tried the chair for a longer period and comfort scores ticked upward, the same people gave the chair extremely low aesthetic ratings. Viewers had difficulty conceptually processing the chair – it did not look like an office chair, and instead was compared by some observers to lawn furniture. Herman Miller could afford to launch a long-term campaign for the aesthetic hearts and minds of office managers. Eventually, after the chair began to win over others in the design world and was featured on movies and television, the aesthetic scores went up. But for years the reaction to the chair was negative because it did not fit the category of "office chair" in observers' heads.[34]

The teachings of the aesthetic middle reveal that the public's taste in design need not be a complete mystery. Particular design features operate to move a design into the aesthetic middle – the sweet spot for a combination of novelty and processing ease. In its current incarnation, design nonobviousness disclaims almost any analysis of prior art or any weighing of the salience of particular design features, instead denying patent protection only when a single virtually identical design can be found. This simplistic analysis stems from a misguided belief that visual design, unlike scientific discovery, cannot tolerate objective comparisons with prior art, save for a superficial check for an identical primary reference. Thanks to a particularly rich array of neuroaesthetic research investigating commercial design preference, much more searching comparisons with other commercial designs are possible. This still begs the question as to whether design patents should promote designs that are pleasing to consumers or designs that appear innovative to designers. Chapter 6 offers an answer as well as more specifics on how to go about comparing a claimed design against what came before.

Notes

1 Smith v. Whitman Saddle Co., 148 U.S. 674, 679 (1893) (agreeing that design patents require "originality and beauty"); Steffens v. Steiner, 232 F. 862, 864 (2d Cir. 1916) ("A design ... is patentable if, as a whole, it produces a new and pleasing impression on the aesthetic sense.").
2 Christopher Buccafusco, *Making Sense of Intellectual Property Law*, 97 Cornell L. Rev. 501, 526 (2012).

[3] Zhihao Zhang et al., *Toward a Neuroscientifically Informed "Reasonable Person" Test* 2–3, https://papers.ssrn.com/sol3/papers.cfm?abstract_id= 3876774.

[4] M. Dorothee Augustin et al., *The Neural Time Course of Art Perception: An ERP Study on the Processing of Style Versus Content in Art*, 49 NEUROPSYCHOLOGIA 2071, 2072 (2011).

[5] E.g., Johan De Smedt & Helen De Cruz, *Toward an Integrative Approach of Cognitive Neuroscientific and Evolutionary Psychological Studies of Art*, 8 EVOLUTIONARY PSYCHOL. 695, 701 (2010); Juan Garcia-Prieto et al., *Neurocognitive Decoding of Aesthetic Appreciation*, in MULTIMODAL OSCILLATION-BASED CONNECTIVITY THEORY 87, 97 (S. Palva ed. 2016).

[6] Garcia-Prieto et al., *supra*, at 100; Edward A. Vessel et al., *Art Reaches Within: Aesthetic Experience, the Self and the Default Mode Network*, 7 FRONTIERS HUM. NEUROSCI. 1, 9 (2013).

[7] Caleb Warren & Martin Reimann, *Crazy-Funny-Cool Theory: Divergent Reactions to Unusual Product Designs*, 4 J. ASSN. CONS. RES. 409, 417 (2019).

[8] Joel Pearson, *The Human Imagination: The Cognitive Neuroscience of Visual Mental Imagery*, 20 NATURE 624, 627–29 (2019).

[9] Joan L. Giese et al., *Advancing the Aesthetic Middle Principle: Trade-Offs in Design Attractiveness and Strength*, 67 J. BUS. RES. 1154, 1159 (2014).

[10] Anthony Chmiel & Emery Schubert, *Back to the Inverted-U for Music Preference: A Review of the Literature*, 45 PSYCH. MUSIC 886, 905 (2017); Wolfram Schultz, *Neuronal Reward and Decision Signals: From Theories to Data*, 95 PHYSIOLOGICAL REV. 853, 853–55 (2015).

[11] Benno Belke et al., *When Challenging Art Gets Liked: Evidences for a Dual Preference Formation Process for Fluent and Non-Fluent Portraits*, 10 PLOS ONE 1, 2 (2015).

[12] Rolf Reber et al., *Processing Fluency and Aesthetic Pleasure: Is Beauty in the Perceiver's Processing Experience?*, 8 PERSONALITY & SOC. PSYCH. REV. 364, 365 (2004).

[13] Laura K.M. Graf et al., *Measuring Processing Fluency: One Versus Five Items*, J. CONS. PSYCH. 393, 394 (2017); Dan King & Chris Janiszewski, *The Sources and Consequences of Fluent Processing of Numbers*, 48 J. MKTG. RES. 327, 336 (2011).

[14] Reber, *supra*, at 372.

[15] P. Andrew Leynes & Richard J. Addante, *Neurophysiological Evidence that Perceptions of Fluency Produce Mere Exposure Effects*, 16 COGNITIVE AFFECT. BEHAV. NEUROSCI. 754, 755 (2016); Joel L. Voss et al., *More Than a Feeling: Pervasive Influences of Memory without Awareness of Retrieval*, 3 COGNITIVE NEUROSCI. 193, 194 (2012). Businesses are already aware of the role of memory and prior exposure in forming aesthetic preference. There is even a name for the phenomenon of convincing consumers of past pleasurable experiences with brands when those experiences never actually took place:

"the false experience effect." See Priyali Rajagopal & Nicole Votolato Montgomery, *I Imagine, I Experience, I Like: The False Experience Effect*, 38 J. Cons. Res. 578, 579 (2011).

[16] Amy M. Belfi et al., *Rapid Timing of Musical Aesthetic Judgments*, 147 J. Exp. Psych: General 1531, 1532–35 (2018).

[17] Graf et al., *supra*, at 395.

[18] Michael Forster et al., *Do I Really Feel It? The Contributions of Subjective Fluency and Compatibility in Low-Level Effects on Aesthetic Appreciation*, 9 Frontiers Hum. Neurosci. 1, 8 (2015).

[19] Reber et al., *supra*, at 366.

[20] Laura K. M. Graf & Jan R. Landwehr, *Aesthetic Pleasure versus Aesthetic Interest: The Two Routes to Aesthetic Liking*, 8 Frontiers Psych. 1, 13 (2017).

[21] Belke et al., *supra*, at 6.

[22] Curver Luxembourg, SARL v. Home Expressions, Inc., 938 F.3d 1334 (Fed. Cir. 2019).

[23] Belke et al., *supra*, at 7.

[24] Bingbing Li et al., *Electrophysiological Signals Associated with Fluency of Different Levels of Processing Reveal Multiple Contributions to Recognition Memory*, 53 Consciousness Cognition 1, 2–3 (2017).

[25] Eline Van Geert & Johan Wagemans, *Order, Complexity, and Aesthetic Appreciation*, 14 Psychol. Aesthetics Creativity & Arts 135, 135 (2020).

[26] Paul Hekkert, *Design Aesthetics: Principles of Pleasure in Design*, 48 Psych. Sci. 157 (2006).

[27] Del Coates, Watches Tell More Than Time: Product Design, Information, and the Quest for Elegance 197–99 (2003).

[28] Moran Cerf et al., *Using Single-Neuron Recording in Marketing: Opportunities, Challenges, and an Application to Fear Enhancement in Communications*, 52 J. Mktg. Res. 530, 534 (2015); Jan Kaminski et al., *Novelty-Sensitive Dopaminergic Neurons in the Human Substantia Nigra Predict Success of Declarative Memory Formation*, 28 Current Biol. 1333, 1340 (2018).

[29] Philippe Chassy et al., *A Relationship between Visual Complexity and Aesthetic Appraisal of Car Front Images: An Eye-Tracker Study*, 44 Perception 1085, 1086 (2015).

[30] Jan R. Landwehr et al., *Product Design for the Long Run: Consumer Responses to Typical and Atypical Designs at Different Stages of Exposure*, 77 J. Mktg. 92, 104 (2013).

[31] Melika Husic-Mehmedovic et al., *Seeing Is Not Necessarily Liking: Advancing Research on Package Design with Eye-Tracking*, 80 J. Bus. Res. 145, 151–52 (2017).

[32] Malcolm Gladwell, Blink: The Power of Thinking without Thinking 169 (2005).

[33] US Patent No. D486, 657S (Feb. 17, 2004).

[34] Gladwell, *supra*, at 168–74.

5   NEUROMARKS

The divide between intellectual property law's armchair theories of human cognition and the revelations from two decades of brain science is particularly noticeable and surprising when it comes to trademark law. Most of the applied research into brain function focuses on the specific question of how shoppers make decisions. Market research, not studies of criminals' grey matter, is where the money is. As discussed in the prior chapter, marketers leverage neuroscience to better understand how consumers appreciate design. They spend even more time and money on using brain science to develop more effective branding strategies. Most large advertising agencies and market research firms now have neuromarketing divisions. Blue-chip companies that have used neural know-how to design advertising campaigns include Volvo, McDonald's, PepsiCo, and Google. Thanks to this emphasis on learning about shoppers' minds, our understanding of consumer thought can only improve in the years to come.

Estimates of consumer thought form the bulk of trademark doctrine. A series of common law rules instantiate judicial intuitions about (1) when potential purchasers are likely to view a word or symbol as indicating the source of goods; and (2) when these purchasers are likely to be confused by the actions of another party. In addition, a federal statute prohibiting "trademark dilution" asks courts to intuit when non-confusing uses of another party's trademark somehow blur or tarnish the signaling power of that trademark inside consumers' heads.

The problem is that even if they could somehow root out their own biases, judges never know exactly what the consumer is thinking. Judges themselves recognize this. In the 1940s, the same judge whose innovations are responsible for many of the current contours of copyright law, Jerome Frank, voiced his desire to replace his "shaky kind of guess" as to the likelihood of trademark confusion with something that better reflected actual consumer sentiment.[1] Frank went so far as to undertake his own market research, questioning a group of "adolescent girls and their mothers and sisters ... chosen at random" to determine whether actual consumers would confuse plaintiff's SEVENTEEN for magazines with defendant's MISS SEVENTEEN for girdles. Frank admitted that "my method of obtaining such data is not satisfactory" but thought it preferable to deciding the issue without consulting anyone of the relevant purchasing class: teenage girls. More recently, Judge Richard Posner acknowledged judicial "blind spots" when it comes to trying to understand consumer behavior.[2]

What if instead of guessing, we could know what consumers are thinking? Consider a study using neural imaging to measure changes in brain blood flow and oxygenation while research subjects viewed several well-known trademarks. Afterwards, the study's participants completed a widely used market research survey designed to assess each brand's personality traits. On the basis of these two data sets, the researchers claimed the ability to decode "the representational space of brand personality in the brain," successfully predicting the brain activity of consumers viewing other trademarks like Disney or Gucci. According to the researchers, each brand has a different neural signature, with different brain regions reflecting perceptions like "excitement," "ruggedness," or "sophistication" upon exposure to the brand stimulus. By viewing these neural signatures, researchers could distinguish whether the subject was thinking about Apple or Microsoft, Coke or Pepsi.[3]

This chapter describes the state of the art in consumer neuroscience and its relationship to the legal questions of distinctiveness, likelihood of confusion, and dilution that dominate trademark law. Businesses are bankrolling experiments and technologies meant to reveal the essential ingredients of buying behavior. A key part of this research searches for the neural hallmarks of successful brands. The chapter then predicts how the estimates of consumer perception that run through trademark law will be altered by neuroscience. Antecedent collisions between law and psychology offer lessons for how neuroscientific understandings may be incorporated into trademark doctrine.

TRADEMARK LAW AND CONSUMER PERCEPTION

For almost any trademark case, the central question at issue is how consumers are likely to perceive a particular advertising stimulus. Take, for example, a 2020 lawsuit initiated by the restaurant chain Panda Express. To seek trademark protection, the restaurant chain needs to demonstrate that its mark is "distinctive," i.e., consumers recognize the PANDA EXPRESS mark as identifying a source of goods or services. To figure out whether consumers interpret a mark as a source identifier, courts employ tests of their own construction such as the "imagination test" (asking if the term at issue requires imagination to reach a conclusion as to the nature of the product) or the "double entendre" test (treating marks that employ twofold meanings as automatically distinctive). If the mark at issue passes these tests – for example, a court concludes that a consumer requires some imagination to discern that the PANDA EXPRESS mark is for a Chinese restaurant and, hence, the mark signals source instead of mere product characteristics – then the mark is considered "inherently distinctive" and enjoys full trademark rights without any proof of actual consumer sentiment.

If a mark fails these tests, however, then the mark proponent must provide evidence of "acquired distinctiveness" in the minds of consumers. Courts look to circumstantial proof like the amount of advertising conducted by the mark proponent, total sales of the relevant product, and evidence that the defendant knowingly imitated the plaintiff's symbol to determine if a mark has acquired distinctiveness. The basic question at issue in the acquired distinctiveness analysis is whether consumers have come to associate the mark at issue with a particular source of goods or services. If PANDA EXPRESS does not indicate source to consumers, it lacks distinctiveness and forfeits trademark protection.

If the owners of Panda Express convince a court that they own a distinctive mark, they can potentially sue others for trademark infringement. In the lawsuit, Panda Express objected to a new Chinese restaurant that styled itself "Panda Libre," contending that Kung Pao chicken fans would confuse the new restaurant with their own. Again, the court must estimate consumer perception, this time asking whether customers will mistake the defendant's trademark for the plaintiff's. The courts rely on a multi-factor test to answer this question. Although the number and nature of the factors differ according to jurisdiction, there is a consensus that the following factors must be part of the consumer confusion analysis:

- similarity of the plaintiff's and defendant's marks
- "strength" of the plaintiff's mark
- intent of the defendant
- purchaser sophistication
- presence of actual confusion
- relatedness of the goods or services at issue.

As these factors make clear, judges assess likelihood of confusion through intuition and proxies for consumer sentiment rather than actual testing of that sentiment. Only the actual confusion factor permits direct evidence of consumer thought to enter the analysis.

Finally, let's assume that a separate party, a portable toilet supplier, begins selling its services under the "Panda Express" name. Even if portable toilet customers are not confused into thinking the two companies are related, the restaurant chain could try to sue for trademark dilution. A court would need to decide whether exposure to the portable toilet mark alters the signaling power of the PANDA EXPRESS mark for Chinese restaurants in consumers' heads.

One variety of the dilution cause of action asks if the defendant's use of the mark somehow harms the reputation of the plaintiff's mark. A court evaluating such a claim would need to assess whether consumers are likely to make a mental association between the plaintiff's and the defendant's marks and whether that association somehow negatively impacts their estimation of the original PANDA EXPRESS mark.

As these hypotheticals about Panda Express demonstrate, judicial estimates of consumer thought dominate trademark law. The problem is that these estimates typically lack empirical grounding. The trier of fact needs to comprehend the collective mind of the consuming public with little to go on but her own sense of what seems distinctive, confusing, or dilutive. Against this background, it is easy to see the appeal of consumer neuroscience for trademark law. It offers the potential for replacing hunches and indirect evidence with direct neural evidence of consumer perception.

EXPLORING THE CONSUMING MIND

Consumer neuroscience uses technologies for studying the brain to reveal "the neural conditions and processes that underlie consumption, their psychological meaning, and their behavioral consequences."[4] From the advertiser's perspective, reliance on neurophysiological data avoids the problems inherent in consumer self-reporting. For a long time, researchers have developed branding strategies based on responses provided through consumer surveys and focus groups. The problem is that shoppers do not always tell the truth. Sometimes they misreport because they do not want to convey something embarrassing or taboo to their interlocutors. At other times, they simply cannot articulate or recognize their own thoughts in relation to an advertising or product stimulus. Some high-profile product introductions, like "New Coke" in the 1980s, were rigorously vetted by sample consumers before their public rollout. Yet they still flopped. Surveyed consumers told market researchers what they wanted to hear instead of sharing their true feelings about the product.[5]

Neuroscientific methods of gauging consumer thought avoid the problem of consumers who don't know or don't want to reveal what is going on in their heads. The number of firms specializing in neuromarketing continues to grow as businesses plow resources into this new kind of market research that avoids some of the traditional problems with consumer self-reporting. As the technology advances, neuroscientists are probing the main drivers of successful branding. Most important for courts deciding trademark disputes, these researchers have pinpointed some of the neural signs of trademark familiarity, comparison, and meaning.

Brand Familiarity

A central point of emphasis for neuromarketing is branding. Neuroscience cemented its unique ability to measure brand equity in a 2004 study. Test subjects took sips of Coke and Pepsi while their heads were in an fMRI scanner. At first, the sipped brand remained hidden and subjects were simply asked to rate each cola's taste. Participants expressed a slight taste preference for Pepsi. Meanwhile, the scanner revealed a heightened response in a region of the brain that mediates pleasure and reward when the subjects drank Pepsi, thus matching the verbalized taste preference. Next, the subjects did the same thing, but this time saw the brand name of the beverage before they took their sips. Seeing the brand name not only triggered a switch in verbal preference (most participants now said they favored the taste of Coke), but also in neural activity. Notifying subjects that they were drinking Coke prompted stronger neural responses in subjects than notifying them that they were drinking Pepsi. The study proved that successful branding not only changes our reported enjoyment of a product, but it can actually change consumer brain chemistry, and this change can be measured.[6]

Since 2004, researchers have built on the Coke study's findings to develop more precise measurements of brand influence in consumers' minds. A great deal of applied research involves figuring out how consumers perceive and retrieve memories of different brands. fMRI and EEG readings can assess how successful an advertiser has been in planting brand impressions in our minds. When a consumer is exposed to a strong brand like Coke, fMRI scanners detect activity in parts of the brain associated with value encoding and familiarity. Research already reveals differences in the firing rates of neurons in two regions of the brain – the hippocampus and the amygdala – based on whether images are being viewed for the first time or have been seen before. "With great specificity and sensitivity, researchers can, on the basis of brain data, determine whether lab subjects have or have not seen particular sets of words and images."[7]

Hence, consumer neuroscience offers the possibility of measuring how deeply a brand is etched into audience memories, information central to trademark law's acquired distinctiveness analysis. According to the neuroscientists doing this work, brain imaging now "provides a direct measure of the strength of encoding during the ad."[8] Current analyses of acquired distinctiveness rely on circumstantial evidence – like sales volume and advertising expenditures – to determine the public's familiarity with a mark. Neural imaging would seem to offer more direct and persuasive evidence of the public's recognition of a trademark.[9]

Confusion and Consumer Choice

Other consumer neuroscience research analyzes the ways consumers make choices. Consumer decision-making typically requires a decision between two (or more) shopping options. Should I buy Toothpaste A or Toothpaste B? Particular regions of the brain show different levels of activation depending on how the consumer is comparing brands. The brain's ventromedial prefrontal cortex processes the emotions involved when deciding between two trademarks. One study demonstrates that this area of the brain exhibits different levels of activation when consumers evaluate advertising geared to brand usefulness as opposed to brand pleasure.[10] Strong brands prompt consumers to emphasize short-term benefits over long-term gains, and different shopping contexts can cause brands to have more or less importance to our buying decisions. One can see how these insights could be useful not just from the perspective of advertising effectiveness, but from a legal perspective. If certain environmental factors cause consumers to be less thoughtful or, in the parlance of trademark law, less "sophisticated," their presence should make confusion more likely.

Researchers also tout "the potential to detect brand confusion" from studying the activity of a single neuron known to respond in a particular way to a particular brand stimulus.[11] The idea seems to be that if Coke has a unique neural signature and a rival usage (e.g., "Koke") triggers that same neural signature in consumers' brains, that could be compelling evidence of consumer confusion. Other research uses the ability to detect declines in neural response after repeated exposure to a stimulus to construct indexes of visual similarity. These indexes can be used to assess the degree of perceived similarity between a business's distinct product packaging and that of a rival using comparable coloring or lettering.[12] If a unique neural signature can be identified for a well-known brand, then an interloper whose mark triggers the similar neural associations in consumers' heads may be accused of infringement.

Admittedly, there is a distinction between recognizing the plaintiff's trademark when viewing the defendant's mark and being confused into thinking that the defendant's mark is the plaintiff's mark. Hence, trademark confusion could not be conclusively demonstrated by showing that consumers exhibited the same neural pattern when viewing the defendant's mark as when they viewed the plaintiff's. At the least, however, evidence of this kind of recognition would be suggestive of confusion. After all, the current likelihood of confusion test considers mark similarity to be extremely probative of confusion. In a sense, the ability to compare brands' neural signatures would offer a richer, more detailed portrait of mark similarity, one that substitutes direct evidence of consumer perception for judicial guesswork.

Brand Meaning

Scientists seek to neurologically test not just brand familiarity, but brand meaning. Even strong brands differ in the meanings they encode in consumers' memories. A vital component of brand meaning is the ability to make a trademark serve as a signifier of status within the consumer's social group. Neuromarketers diagnose certain areas of the brain that exhibit increased activity when a brand successfully signals status to a consumer.[13] Brain activity can also indicate when a brand is "culturally familiar" to a particular demographic. For example, when German test subjects were presented with different luxury car logos (e.g., BMW vs. Acura), a particular region of the prefrontal cortex was activated only by the culturally familiar logos.[14] Neuroscience studies also reveal that exposure to brands with reputations for style or creativity prompts consumers to behave more impulsively.[15]

Researchers identify neural traits for categories even more specific than "status brands," "culturally familiar brands," or "creative brands." As described by one group of consumer neuroscientists, the research is at the stage where "the brands a consumer is thinking about can be reliably predicted from patterns of neural activations."[16] Just by showing consumers brand names and looking at the resulting fMRI measurements, neuroscientists were able to tell whether the consumer was thinking about Louis Vuitton or Coca-Cola, IBM or Google.

Patterns of brain activity can even be translated into brand personality traits, revealing that consumers think of Campbell's Soup as "sincere," Ford as "rugged," and Mercedes-Benz as "sophisticated."[17] Such research promises to reveal not just the degree of consumer recognition of a trademark, but how consumers feel about and understand the brand at issue.

Assessments of brand meaning bear on actions for trademark dilution that require courts to determine whether a defendant's non-confusing use of a similar mark harms the reputation of the plaintiff's mark. To date, the difficulty in determining whether an "association" will develop in the consumer's head after witnessing the defendant's unauthorized use of a famous mark has limited the viability of the dilution cause of action. Also difficult is assessing the reputational effects of such an association. Better insight into brand meaning could change this. If a perceived brand meaning can be determined through neural scans, then it seems plausible that changes to that meaning in response to the defendant's mark can be assessed as well.

Limitations

Some final words of caution are appropriate when considering consumer neuroscience's potential. fMRI and EEG results undoubtedly reveal a wealth of information about consumer thought. At the same time, the meaning of this information is not always apparent. There is a certain amount of subjectivity inherent in the reading of brain scans; it is not always clear how an influx of blood or electrical impulses to a particular neural territory should be interpreted. The consumer memories and emotions that translate into brand distinctiveness and brand meaning involve complex processes occurring across the entire brain, not just one neural area. While it is fairly clear that particular emotional responses (e.g., pain, fear, happiness) activate different regions in the brain, it is not so clear that when one of these regions is activated, a researcher can infer that a particular emotional state has been reached. This means that consumer neuroscientists have work to do before they can claim evidence of one legally significant mental state like confusion versus another like mere recognition.

Another objection might be to the ability of researchers to identify an empirically sound baseline for consumer perception of a particular brand. Imaging capabilities need to be sufficiently precise so that two rivals sharing a reputation for "ruggedness" (think truck sellers Dodge and Ford) could be distinguished from each other. There is also the problem of a brand's meaning evolving over time, both intentionally and unintentionally. Strategic decisions to change selling strategies, e.g., moving from a luxury brand model to more of a low-price model, would undoubtedly change consumer perceptions of the brand at issue. Even choosing to extend a brand into different territories, say from packaged foods to housewares, could modify a mark's neural signature. The Pierre Cardin trademark once had a reputation for glamour, but rampant licensing of the name on everything from frying pans to sardines reshaped consumer associations. Covid, the name of a longstanding global distributor of audiovisual equipment, meant one thing to consumers in 2019 and something far different by 2020.[18] If neural recordings of brand perception are inherently unstable, one might question their value as a tool for detecting changes in mark reputation and assessing consumer confusion.

Both of these concerns deserve weight in evaluating the current probative value of neuroscientific evidence for trademark law. But it is also important to realize that neuroscientists, cognizant of these criticisms, are taking them into account. Researchers are becoming more adept at discerning multiregional brain activity that describes a unique cognitive condition. For example, a study employing such an approach was able to predict with a high degree of accuracy whether subjects were in a "knowing" mental state versus a "reckless" one – categories that are often criticized for being hard to differentiate yet triggering dramatically different punishments under criminal law.[19] By examining a variety of brain regions at once, consumer neuroscientists can already pinpoint differences in neural signatures among closely related brands like Coke and Pepsi and Apple and Microsoft. As the technology and understanding of the brain advances, the ability to make fine-grained distinctions between consumer perceptions of a mark's attributes should improve.

Admittedly, brand meanings change, which means the timing of when a neural snapshot is taken and submitted into evidence in a trademark case will be critical. But this is an issue that trademark law already has to negotiate. Courts accept survey evidence predating the defendant's allegedly infringing use, reasoning that such evidence can be relevant while also considering timing in determining the survey's ultimate value. A plaintiff that tried to offer evidence of changes to its brand reputation based on the defendant's activity would lose credibility if its neural evidence of the brand's baseline reputation was years out of date. In addition, defendants would be free to refute such stale evidence by conducting their own, more up-to-date neural imaging tests.

It is true that all of the consumer neuroscience research discussed thus far can only supply information on general propensities, not absolute indications of legally relevant mental characteristics for a specific individual. But, like copyright and patent law, trademark law does not worry itself with the mental state of a single actor. It is the aggregate sense of likely consumer thought that determines whether or not a trademark is protectable or infringement has taken place. In this way, neuroscience has greater potential applicability to trademark law than other legal subject areas.

NEUROSCIENCE'S LIKELY PATH IN TRADEMARK CASES

How will trademark law actually respond to a changing scientific understanding of the consuming mind? Any application of new discoveries about consumer thought to the law will have to be negotiated. Just as there is a problem with assuming that neuroscience will transform criminal law, it is unlikely that neuroscience will uproot the distinctiveness and likelihood of confusion analyses – linchpins of trademark litigation that have existed in relatively the same form for over forty years. They afford judges a tremendous amount of discretion, which would be forfeit if junked in favor of fMRI results.

Instead, we need to look for potential reforms to trademark law that would operate in Kalven's middle range – the terrain residing between deeply held values and well-known factual propositions that is susceptible to the influence of social science evidence. Better understanding of consumer thought processes can alter legal premises that represent neither unshakeable legal theory nor generally received wisdom. The story of how psychologist-approved surveys of consumer confusion were first introduced into trademark cases offers an instructive example.

The Story of Surveys

In the early twentieth century, reformers called for replacing the ad hoc "judicial estimate of the state of the public mind" with psychologist expert testimony in trademark cases.[20] The most concrete and lasting innovation proposed by the reformers was to use expert-led consumer surveys to demonstrate confusion. Multiple psychologists contended that their expertise was needed to rein in a body of law being mis-handled by untrained judges.[21]

Rather than being offended by the psychologists' presumption to tell the judiciary how to do their job, a federal appeals court cited an academic psychologist's results to admit that judicial assays of confusion "failed to match the response of ordinary consumers."[22] Other courts agreed to shore up their analysis by admitting in as evidence the surveys of consumer confusion conducted by psychologists. Not every judge welcomed the intrusion of outside authorities into an area that had traditionally been within their sole discretion. Nevertheless, the overall trend was one of more and more surveys being admitted into evidence.

Over time, surveys became a critical component of modern trade-mark law. The early skepticism over such evidence largely vanished. Today, surveys have reached a level of reliability such that they are routinely admitted to guide the determination of trademark disputes. Although some empirical studies suggest that survey evidence plays a less-than-decisive role in the majority of trademark infringement deci-sions, the research also shows that surveys strongly influence the infringement analysis when introduced and are employed widely in the pretrial stages of trademark litigation.[23] In addition to surveying confusion, modern experts provide surveys relating to mark distinct-iveness, strength, and dilution. Scholars in other legal disciplines have noticed, describing trademark law's favorable treatment of surveys as placing it at the vanguard of incorporating social science evidence into adjudication.[24]

The admission of survey evidence of consumer perception fits within Kalven's middle range where social science can influence the law. The survey evidence proffered by early twentieth-century psychologists did not purport to uproot a deeply held legal premise. It simply provided evidence of "actual confusion," albeit in an artificial setting, not the actual marketplace. The results of these surveys tended to support rather than erode a general preference for strong trademark rights. Their admission into evidence seemed very much in keeping with the goals of trademark law.

Notably, other attempts by psychologists to change legal doctrine in this era foundered when judges deemed the evidence proffered as mere common sense. For example, psychologists offering advice on witness veracity in the early twentieth century seemed to present a solution to a problem that did not exist. After all, judges already considered themselves (and the juries they instructed) adept at assessing the credibility of witnesses. Trademark survey evidence differed in that it purported to measure the thought processes of not just one person, but the entire consuming public. Although judges and juries routinely assessed the mental states of individual defendants, there was less comfort with having the trier of fact speak for an entire mass of shoppers. Meanwhile, early twentieth-century psychologists professed a unique ability to study consumer thought "under laboratory conditions."[25]

Consumer neuroscience evidence may work its way into trademark law in a similar fashion as survey evidence. At least in the near term, it will not replace judicial estimates of consumer perception. But it will influence those estimates and, as a result, affect specific areas of trademark law. These probable areas of influence can be divided into three areas: supplementing survey evidence, altering the confusion factors, and expanding the scope of trademark dilution.

Supplementing Surveys

As its reliability increases, like survey evidence, neural indications of a trademark's acquired distinctiveness and consumer confusion are likely to be accepted into evidence in trademark cases. Consumer neuroscientists can claim a core professional competence lacked by judges. Instead of simply reflecting "common sense," fMRI imaging offers evidence of consumer thought "in situations in which consumers are unlikely to say what they think, because they can't or they won't."[26] Rather than challenging an essential value in trademark law, neuroimaging's proponents can follow in the path of consumer surveys and promise a supplement for understanding consumer perception. The premium already placed on expert-led surveys of distinctiveness and confusion should favorably predispose courts to the admission of neuroscientific evidence on these issues.

One might question the need for neuroscientific evidence of acquired distinctiveness and confusion given the consumer behavioral studies that are already submitted to courts in the form of survey data. In fact, persistent reliability problems with survey evidence make a neuroscientific supplement desirable. Surveys requesting a consumer's verbal response to whether or not a symbol indicates the source of a product can be flawed and trigger misleading responses. A survey respondent may be prompted to view a mark that merely describes a product's qualities (e.g., COLD AND CREAMY for ice cream) as a source identifier from the call of the question rather than her own unbiased perception of the mark. For example, to ascertain acquired distinctiveness, surveys often present consumers with a descriptive mark and then immediately ask: "Does this [mark] identify any particular brands, products, or companies to you or not?"[27] One may wonder whether the respondent would have matched the mark with any brand or product if not for the question's prompting. Similar concerns can limit the influence of survey evidence of consumer confusion.

By contrast, neuroimaging results offer the same benefit for courts assessing consumer perception that they do for market researchers: the promise of a consumer's unfiltered, immediate responses to an advertising stimulus, without falsehoods or answers that the respondent thinks the questioner wants to hear. Brain scans do not even require a question to be asked. Test subjects can simply be shown the plaintiff's and defendant's marks and their resulting brain activity analyzed. As a result, two sources of bias are seemingly ameliorated through neurological scans of consumers: that of consumers failing to reveal their "true" impressions of a mark and that of survey administrators, whether accidentally or by design, skewing the results through their interrogation of respondents. In a move reminiscent of psychologists critiquing early twentieth-century judges for their assays of consumer sentiment, neuroscientists tout their superior ability to surface consumer thought as a way to audit traditional survey evidence for potential bias.[28]

Admittedly, both surveys and neurological scans of consumers can be attacked for not replicating real-world shopping conditions or for failing to sample individuals within the relevant purchasing class. To be probative, a consumer experiment must recreate the essential shopping experience. And, for the most part, trademark law only concerns itself with likely purchasers of the items at issue. Surveys that inaccurately reflect the marketplace or sample the wrong consumer universe may be declared inadmissible. Yet if these concerns have not prevented all consumer surveys from being accepted into evidence, it is unlikely that they will prevent neuroimaging results from being accepted into evidence either. Indeed, as neural imaging technologies become more portable, it will become easier to simulate the shopping environments actually encountered by consumers.

In the last two chapters, I suggested that neuroaesthetic evidence would prompt changes to the ways in which courts predict audience responses for copyright and design patent law, but that such evidence would not be admitted to help decide individual cases. Trademark law seems more likely to actually allow some neuroscientific experiments into evidence. Although both have baffled them for decades, judges seem to consider audience perception of commercial information less mysterious than audience reactions to art. Moreover, even if there remain some valid concerns about the accuracy of consumer neuroscience evidence, it bears repeating that even flawed scientific techniques can find their way into the courtroom. I have tried to document the limitations to consumer neuroscience that might make one question its evidentiary role in trademark cases. Yet stacked against those limitations are precedents in trademark law for the admission of outside evidence of consumer perception and continuing investments and technological advances that will only increase the ability of neural imaging to shed light on consumer behavior.

Reprioritizing the Confusion Factors

In contrast to offering evidence relevant to established legal doctrine (e.g., the presence of actual confusion among consumers), neuroscience will also change that doctrine. Neural imaging will likely reshape how trademark law defines consumer confusion and dilution, but in somewhat subtle ways likely to redound to the benefit of trademark holders.

Courts routinely caution that application of the various likelihood of confusion factors is meant to be flexible and the weight given to any particular factor can adjust to the circumstances of each case. The unsettled state of the factors offers opportunity for doctrinal reform. Some of the likelihood of confusion factors (actual confusion and mark strength) are likely to take on more salience when amplified by neurological measurement. Others (similarity of the marks, relatedness of goods or services, and defendant's intent) will probably decline in importance.

As consumer neuroscience develops, the actual confusion factor may become more important to the likelihood of confusion analysis. This factor looks at evidence of consumer confusion under actual marketplace conditions, whether in the form of anecdotal evidence from real customers of the plaintiff or defendant or in the form of surveys of the relevant class of prospective customers for the goods or services at issue. Already, the direct nature of actual confusion evidence, as opposed to the indirect evidence that comprises the rest of the likelihood of confusion factors, exerts a strong pull on judges. According to one federal court, "There can be no more positive or substantial proof of the likelihood of confusion than proof of actual confusion."[29] Consumer neuroscientists can see what a consumer's brain looks like when it views a particular trademark, and they can potentially look for the same pattern when consumers see an allegedly infringing mark. At the level of doctrine, the admission of such evidence is likely to make the actual confusion factor loom even larger in the judicial imagination.

The mark strength factor will take on greater weight in the likelihood of confusion analysis as well. Every federal court assesses the strength of the plaintiff's mark as part of its calculation of whether consumers are likely to be confused by the defendant's actions. Mark strength is a question of distinctiveness: the more strength a mark has, the "more consumers who use the mark as a source identifier."[30] Consumer neuroscientists are getting more skilled at being able to measure the ability of brands to capture attention and remain in memory. Mark strength is already central to likelihood of confusion.[31] It may become even more important once it appears susceptible to direct measurement through fMRI and EEG readings.

By contrast, other parts of the confusion analysis that do not offer a direct measurement of actual consumer perception may recede in importance once images and data from neural scans are admitted into evidence. It makes eminent sense to consider mark similarity and relatedness of goods in evaluating the potential for confusion. But courts have wrestled for decades with the degree of similarity and relatedness needed to confuse consumers. In applying these factors, the trier of fact is placed in the uncomfortable position of trying to channel consumer thought. It takes a certain amount of chutzpah for one person in black robes to decide whether consumers will perceive the "Panda Express" and "Panda Libre" marks similarly. Although some courts seem to have great faith in their ability to make this sort of judgment, others are less sanguine. As one court noted: "the most successful form of [trademark] copying is to employ enough points of similarity to confuse the public with enough points of difference to confuse the courts."[32] Already mistrustful of their own guesses as to which mark resemblances strike too close to home, courts may be even less tempted to rely on these guesses when they can place their faith in tangible neural evidence of actual confusion.

The confusion factor most likely to suffer from trademark law's neural turn is the defendant's intent. As neural evidence of confusion becomes more compelling, intent's role as a proxy for infringement seems likely to wane. Arguably, intent is indirectly relevant to confusion because of the probability that a defendant who wants to sow the seeds of trademark confusion will be successful in doing so. But this is a very speculative justification. Just because the defendant intends to confuse consumers, there is no reason to believe that the defendant will accomplish its intended goal. As direct neuroscientific evidence of actual confusion and mark strength makes those factors appear more reliable, the unreliable nature of the defendant's intent factor will stand out even more.

Expanding Dilution

Trademark dilution requires a demonstration of one of two different mental phenomena. *Dilution by blurring* demands proof that the similarity between the defendant's and plaintiff's marks is likely to impair the distinctiveness of the plaintiff's mark. *Dilution by tarnishment* necessitates a showing that an association is likely to arise between the defendant's and plaintiff's marks that "harms the reputation" of the plaintiff's mark.[33] Like the distinctiveness and infringement inquiries, dilution doctrine depends on a series of judicial speculations about consumer cognition.

Much like the likelihood of confusion analysis, the dilution by blurring analysis requires courts to march through a set of factors. As with likelihood of confusion, courts are likely to place increased weight on those factors that appear susceptible to direct neural proof. For example, one factor is the existence of "any actual association" between the plaintiff's and the defendant's marks. Determining what constitutes proof of actual association has long perplexed courts hearing dilution cases. Dilution represents a subconscious, spontaneous process that can be hard to measure through the considered responses of survey participants.[34] In the future, however, association evidence could come in the form of neuroscientific studies where consumers were exposed to the defendant's mark and then scrutinized for evidence of brain activity matching the encoding of the plaintiff's mark. Such evidence would seem to avoid a frequent criticism of survey evidence: respondents' inability to say what they really think. With better direct evidence of association, the "actual association" factor might assume the same importance that the "actual confusion" factor already does in the likelihood of confusion analysis.

But consumer neuroscience's largest doctrinal impact may be in the way it changes the cause of action for dilution by tarnishment. It is impossible to assess whether a mark's reputation has been harmed without establishing a baseline for what that reputation is. Courts in dilution cases have responded to this difficulty by limiting the dilution by tarnishment cause of action to use of the famous mark with sex-related products. Use of a famous mark in products involving sex or nudity, according to the courts, triggers negative connotations in consumers' brains.[35] Other uses do not.[36] The rationale seems to be that harm to reputation can be presumed in one particular circumstance because of the supposed power of sexual imagery to shape our thinking.

Dilution by tarnishment has been not only difficult to define, but also difficult to measure, which may be one reason for the doctrinal fixation on sexually related mark uses and a refusal to countenance a variety of other potentially tarnishing conduct. If neuroscience makes brand reputation more transparent, however, that could change. Brain mapping that defines a unique brand personality existing in consumers' heads could establish a reputational baseline. Subsequent changes to this baseline after exposure to the defendant's mark could be cited as evidence of tarnishment. For example, a consumer neuroscience expert might demonstrate that VOLVO stands for safety in a substantial percentage of consumers' minds and that the neural signature for safety diminishes after the introduction of VOLVO chainsaws. Or Panda Express may introduce fMRI scans showing that public perception of its mark changed for the worse after the introduction of Panda Libre porta potties.

For some, using neuroscience to assess brand reputation might sound fantastic. It would seem that the complex web of associations we form over the course of our lives in relation to one particular commercial symbol would be difficult to neurologically test and vary widely from person to person. Yet finding generalizable neural associations for particular brand attributes is exactly what consumer neuroscientists claim to be able to do. By examining not just localized neural activity, but "correlated activity across a network of brain regions," researchers discovered "highly distinctive associations," even among similar brands like Apple and Microsoft. Perhaps even more impressive, these neural measurements of brand personality traits stay relatively constant across samples from different populations with "different demographic and socioeconomic characteristics."[37] According to researchers, tests to determine how marketing actions affect "the mental map of brand personality" are "a natural next step."[38] With the ability to see tangible signs of mark reputation in consumers' brains, courts may be emboldened to recognize tarnishment from more than just sexualized uses of a plaintiff's famous mark. Gradually adding to the small list of potentially tarnishing product areas would not eliminate a cause of action or fundamentally remake dilution law. Instead, it would be a discrete expansion, falling into Kalven's middle range where judges allow psychology to shape legal doctrine.

To summarize, consumer neuroscience could reshape trademark law in a number of ways. Neuroscientific studies of acquired distinctiveness and confusion may be admitted into evidence. At the least, these studies could act as a check on the reliability of traditional consumer surveys. The neuroscientific turn may cause courts to revise the trademark infringement analysis by privileging likelihood of confusion factors susceptible to direct neural evidence, like mark strength and actual confusion. Perhaps most significant, by promising a biological measurement of mark reputation, neural scans will open the door to broader recognition of dilution by tarnishment beyond unauthorized uses relating to sex. The critical question – addressed later in the book – is whether any of these likely changes would actually be good for trademark law.

Notes

[1] Triangle Publications, Inc. v. Rohrlich, 167 F.2d 969, 976 (2d Cir. 1948).

[2] Kraft Foods Grp. Brands LLC v. Cracker Barrel Old Country Store, Inc., 735 F.3d 735, 741 (7th Cir. 2013).

[3] Yu-Ping Chen et al., *From "Where" to "What": Distributed Representations of Brand Associations in the Human Brain*, 52 J. MKTG. RES. 453, 455 (2015).

[4] Martin Reimann et al., *Functional Magnetic Resonance Imaging Consumer Research: A Review and Application*, 28 PSYCH. & MKTG. 608, 610 (2011).

[5] R.M. Schindler, *The Real Lesson of New Coke: The Value of Focus Groups for Predicting the Effects of Social Influence*, 4 MKTG. RES. 22, 22–27 (1992).

[6] Samuel M. McClure et al., *Neural Correlates of Behavioral Preference for Culturally Familiar Drinks*, 44 NEURON 379, 379 (2004). Aspects of McClure's study have been replicated by other researchers. Michael Koenigs & Daniel Tranel, *Prefrontal Cortex Damage Abolishes Brand-Cued Changes in Cola Preference*, 3 SOC. COGNITIVE AFFECTIVE NEUROSCI. 1, 1–6 (2008).

[7]   Francis X. Shen, *Law and Neuroscience 2.0*, 48 ARIZ. ST. L.J. 1043, 1065 (2016). See also Jesse Rissman et al., *Decoding fMRI Signatures of Real-World Autobiographical Memory Retrieval*, 28 J. COGNITIVE NEUROSCI. 604, 616 (2016) (finding that it is possible to decode from brain activity with a high degree of certainty whether a person recognizes a face or life-event as previously encountered or instead perceives it as novel).

[8]   Vinod Venkatraman et al., *Predicting Advertising Success Beyond Traditional Measures: New Insights from Neurological Methods and Market Response Modeling*, 52 J. MKTG. RES. 436, 440 (2015).

[9]   It is less likely that consumer neuroscience can shed light on the analysis of inherent distinctiveness. While assessing whether consumers have a memory of a particular commercial stimulus seems firmly within neuroscientists' grasp, the mental processes at work in determining whether a trademark automatically indicates that it is a source of goods are more complicated.

[10] Sam O. Al-Kwifi, *The Role of fMRI in Detecting Attitude Toward Brand Switching: An Exploratory Study Using High Technology Products*, 25 J. PRODUCT & BRAND MGMT. 208, 212–13 (2016).

[11] Moran Cerf et al, *Using Single-Neuron Recording in Marketing: Opportunities, Challenges, and an Application to Fear Enhancement in Communications*, 52 J. MKTG. RES. 530, 534 (2015).

[12] Zhihao Zhang et al., *Toward a Neuroscientifically Informed "Reasonable Person" Test* 2–3, https://papers.ssrn.com/sol3/papers.cfm?abstract_id=3876774.

[13] Christopher N. Cascio, *Neural Correlates of Susceptibility to Group Opinions in Online Word-of-Mouth Recommendations*, 52 J. MKTG. RES. 559, 560 (2015); Michael Schaefer & Michael Rotte, *Thinking on Luxury or Pragmatic Brand Products: Brain Responses to Different Categories of Culturally Based Brands*, 1165 BRAIN RES. 98, 101–02 (2007).

[14] Michael Schaefer et al., *Neural Correlates of Culturally Familiar Brands of Car Manufacturers*, 31 NEUROIMAGE 861 (2006).

[15] Carsten Murawski et al., *Led Into Temptation? Rewarding Brand Logos Bias the Neural Encoding of Incidental Economic Decisions*, 7 PLOS ONE 1, 5–6 (2012).

[16] Colin Camerer & Carolyn Yoon, *Introduction to the* Journal of Marketing Research *Special Issue on Neuroscience and Marketing*, 52 J. MKTG. RES. 423, 424 (2015).

[17] Chen et al., *supra*, at 455–58. Other studies complement these neuroscientific assessments of brand personality by looking for response latencies when brands are paired with positive and negative words. See, e.g., Claudiu V. Dimofte, *Implicit Measures of Consumer Cognition: A Review*, 27 PSYCH. & MKTG. 921, 925–28 (2010).

[18] *When Your Company Is Named Covid, You've Heard All the Jokes*, WEEKEND EDITION, May 15, 2021, https://www.npr.org/2021/05/15/994996890/when-your-company-is-named-covid-youve-heard-all-the-jokes.

[19] Iris Vilares et al., *Predicting the Knowledge-Recklessness Distinction in the Human Brain*, 114 PROC. NAT'L ACAD. SCI. 3222 (2017).

[20] FRANK SCHECHTER, THE HISTORICAL FOUNDATIONS RELATING TO THE LAW OF TRADE-MARKS 166 (1925); Edward S. Rogers, *The Unwary Purchaser*, 8 MICH. L. REV. 613, 617 (1910).

[21] HUGO MUNSTERBERG, PSYCHOLOGY AND INDUSTRIAL EFFICIENCY 285 (1913); Harold E. Burtt, *Measurement of Confusion between Similar Trade Names*, 19 ILL. L. REV. 320, 336 (1924); Edward S. Rogers, *An Account of Some Psychological Experiments on the Subject of Trademark Infringement*, 18 MICH. L. REV. 75, 77 (1919).

[22] La Touraine Coffee Co. v. Lorraine Coffee Co., 157 F.2d 115, 124 (2d Cir. 1946).

[23] Robert C. Bird & Joel H. Steckel, *The Role of Consumer Surveys in Trademark Infringement: Empirical Evidence from the Federal Courts*, 14 U. PA. J. BUS. L. 1013, 1041 (2012); Shari Seidman Diamond & David J. Franklyn, *Trademark Surveys: An Undulating Path*, 92 TEX. L. REV. 2029, 2062 (2014).

[24] James E. Ryan, *The Limited Influence of Social Science Evidence in Modern Desegregation Cases*, 81 N.C. L. REV. 1659, 1681–82 (2003).

[25] Burtt, *supra*, at 335.

[26] Uma R. Karmarkar et al., *Marketers Should Pay Attention to fMRI*, HARVARD BUS. REV., Nov. 3, 2015.

[27] David H.B. Bednall et al., *Color, Champagne, and Trademark Secondary Meaning Surveys*, 102 TRADEMARK REP. 967, 999 (2012).

[28] Zhang et al., *supra*.

[29] World Carpets, Inc. v. Dick Littrell's New World Carpets, 438 F.2d 482, 489 (5th Cir. 1971). Although artificial constructs, consumer surveys are typically classified as "actual confusion" evidence. See Water Pik, Inc. v. Med-Systems, Inc., 726 F.3d 1136, 1144 (10th Cir. 2013).

[30] Robert G. Bone, *Taking the Confusion Out of "Likelihood of Confusion": Toward a More Sensible Approach to Trademark Infringement*, 106 NW. U. L. REV. 1307, 1346 (2012). In determining mark strength, courts actually consider two things. The more inherently distinctive the mark, the greater strength it is considered to have and the more likelihood there is of confusion. Thus, a court's previous analysis of distinctiveness is also imported into the likelihood of confusion analysis. Courts also consider a mark's "market strength," relying on many of the factors one reviews in an analysis of acquired distinctiveness (e.g., total sales, amount spent on advertising). Again, the more market strength a mark has, the more likely it is that a court will find the defendant's activity involving that mark as confusing to consumers. Hence, to the extent neuroscientific evidence alters the distinctiveness analysis, it will alter the mark strength calculation as well.

[31] Barton Beebe, *An Empirical Study of the Multifactor Tests for Trademark Infringement*, 94 CALIF. L. REV. 1581, 1636–37 (2006).

[32] Baker v. Master Printers Union, 34 F. Supp. 808, 811 (D.N.J. 1940).

[33] 15 U.S.C. § 1125(c)(2)(B)–(C).

[34] See Shari Seidman Diamond, *Surveys in Dilution Cases II*, *in* TRADEMARK AND DECEPTIVE ADVERTISING SURVEYS: LAW, SCIENCE, AND DESIGN 155, 157–62 (Shari Seidman Diamond & Jerre B. Swann eds., 2012) (discussing the difficulties of producing surveys that measure spontaneous association and assess whether association is likely to impair distinctiveness of a mark). The problem is that this evidence often seems to beg the question. For example, a court credited a survey finding that 87 percent of respondents said "Nike" when asked "What if anything, came to your mind when I first said the word Nikepal?" as evidence of actual association. Nike, Inc. v. Nikepal Intern., Inc., 2007 WL 2782030, *4 (E.D. Cal. 2007). One might object that, rather than revealing actual consumer perception, such a question predisposes respondents to find an association.

[35] V Secret Catalogue v. Moseley, 605 F.3d 382, 386 (6th Cir. 2010).

[36] Note, Jordana S. Loughran, *Tarnishment's Goody-Two-Shoes Shouldn't Get All the Protection: Balancing Trademark Dilution Through Burnishment*, 21 LEWIS & CLARK L. REV. 453, 484 (2017).

[37] Chen et al., *supra*, at 459.

[38] *Id.*

PART III

Using Neuroscience to Improve Intellectual Property Law

6 HOW TO TAKE CREATIVITY SERIOUSLY

Armed with a working knowledge of both legal and neuroscientific construction of the mental processes of creators and audiences, we can move on to a discussion of how and whether to bring science and law into greater alignment. Our exploration of the law of copyright and design patents revealed that intellectual property law's assumptions about creative thought do not match the actual mechanics of the creative process. Before adjusting the law to reflect the realities of creative thought, however, we need to further interrogate the advantages of a meaningful creativity threshold. Some maintain that legal scrutiny of the author's creativity should be replaced by the simpler and more achievable aim of furthering the production of all works, creative or not. Such an approach fails to acknowledge the text of the US Constitution, the costs of ceding the creativity determination to market forces, and the structural benefits to judicial decision-making from the presence of a meaningful creativity test. Once the biological realities of the creative process are acknowledged, authorial motivation and expertise can be used to diagnose the presence of copyright's "creative spark" and the lessons of the aesthetic middle leveraged to set an appropriate baseline against which to evaluate innovation in visual design.

SHOULD NOTHING BE CREATIVE?

For a committed few, "creativity should be banned from the copyright analysis."[1] The primary worry for these creativity abolitionists is an old one: courts must avoid the temptation to aesthetically discriminate between works and even a weak creativity requirement is far too tempting. To avoid bias, the argument goes, courts should get out of the creativity business altogether and simply let the marketplace determine which kinds of expressive works are of value. According to one creativity critic, "[t]he purpose of copyright is to encourage the production of economically valuable works of authorship, not creativity."[2] This is the same argument Justice Holmes marshalled so effectively in *Bleistein* when he wrote it would be a "dangerous undertaking" for lawyers "to constitute themselves final judges of the worth" of expressive content.

Along somewhat similar lines, in a groundbreaking article from 2010, law professor Jeanne Fromer approved of copyright's current subjective definition of creativity. She used psychological studies of the time to suggest that audiences value divergent thinking, which is "personal and subjective," in art whereas they value convergent thinking, which requires convergence on an objective answer to a research question, for science and engineering. Fromer acknowledged that the modern creativity standard is vague and could use more articulation, but, given public sentiment, she resisted any heightening of the creativity threshold for copyright protection. At its heart, Fromer's point was similar to that of the creativity abolitionists in that she called for the creativity requirement to be aligned with the tastes of the marketplace. In her view, copyright's minimal creativity requirement was adequate because audiences prefer subjectivity and personality in their art but without too much "newness."[3]

There are a few problems with the position of the creativity abolitionists. Perhaps foremost, there is a strong argument that the US Constitution requires creativity for copyright eligibility. The Intellectual Property Clause of the Constitution grants Congress the power "[t]o promote the Progress of Science and useful Arts, by securing for limited Times to Authors and Inventors the exclusive Right to their respective Writings and Discoveries."[4] In *Feist*, the Supreme Court deemed the words "authors" and "writings" to both have creative components, leading the Court to demand "a modicum of creativity" for copyright protection. Hence, even if one believes that the creativity requirement is wrongheaded, copyright law is stuck with it.

Leaving the text of the Constitution aside, society profits from promoting the production of works with a high degree of creativity in two main ways. Such works prompt greater advancements in arts, literature, and related endeavors than low originality works. Also, a high creativity standard reduces the cost for aspiring authors and designers to produce their own works by limiting the number and scope of prior expressive assets under copyright and patent protection that they must create around. Allowing only audience taste to set the standard for creativity jeopardizes both of these benefits.

Most importantly, objective measurement of several aspects of the creative process is now realizable in a way that was not possible even a short time ago. To the extent it examined the psychological literature on the creative process at all, prior legal scholarship cited research that depended on the self-reporting of research subjects. While such reports are not per se unreliable, observable data about the creative process realized through neuroscience provide a different perspective, unlocking realities about that process that creators cannot articulate themselves. Recent work reveals both divergent and convergent thinking are important to all creative activities, not just work in the arts or discoveries in the sciences.[5] Even if it is true that audiences currently prefer their science objective and their art subjective, that may only be due to a failure of public imagination given the historical inability to objectively measure artistic creativity.

SHOULD EVERYTHING BE CREATIVE?

A slightly different objection to the creativity requirement does not so much reject creativity's importance as question the need for a specific creativity threshold test. According to this line of attack, it does not matter if there is an ineffectual creativity requirement so long as courts reach the right result through other means. By employing the infringement analysis, copyright's fair use defense, or other areas of intellectual property doctrine to permit copying of uncreative materials, the argument goes, courts can incentivize creative expression while preserving room to create for downstream authors. For example, rather than denying copyright in an alphabetically ordered phone book for lack of creativity, courts should utilize the infringement and fair use analyses to permit others to copy the phone book without penalty. In other words, why not let everything be copyrightable? Similarly, some advocate for granting patents in almost all claimed designs, but then reviewing any allegations of infringement under those patents with a skeptical eye. They contend that it is better to focus on the infringement part of any patent litigation, where the trier of fact can compare the claimed design with the purported infringing design and gain a better sense of the relative values of each design, than to spend much effort on the threshold issue of nonobviousness.[6]

One problem with this approach is it ignores the effects of threshold tests on other areas of the law. In the anatomy of an intellectual property lawsuit, the various parts of that lawsuit – establishing the eligibility of the plaintiff's work for protection, evaluating whether the defendant's work is infringing, examining whether the defendant's work meets the criteria for any applicable defenses – are interdependent. A flawed or non-existent eligibility evaluation infects other components of the litigation.

Infringement, whether of a copyrighted work or a patented design, requires an analysis of whether two works are "substantially similar." The term "similarity" lacks content on its own. The trier of fact needs to ascertain the protectable elements in the original work so it can compare them to the defendant's work and make an infringement determination.[7] As a result, the threshold tests for assessing the plaintiff's eligibility for copyright or patent protection have a role to play in weighing liability for a defendant's conduct. Determining whether the defendant's use comes within the legal scope of the plaintiff's rights necessitates some definition of what those rights are.

The same is true of copyright's fair use defense. One factor of the defense examines the "nature of the copyrighted work," narrowing the scope of fair use for unauthorized use of "highly creative" copyrighted works and broadening it for use of more factual works.[8] All things being equal, it should be more difficult to successfully claim fair use when borrowing from an innovative work. This makes the fair use defense dependent on the trier of fact's estimation of the plaintiff's creative contribution. A scrupulous eligibility determination reduces the amount of analysis required in the infringement and fair use evaluations, but an ineffectual creativity test makes the other parts of copyright law do all the work.[9]

A legal decision that aptly illustrates the structural problems with today's minimalist creativity requirement is *Conan Properties v. Mattel.*[10] Conan Properties (CPI) held copyright in several comic books published in the 1970s featuring the character of Conan the Barbarian. CPI could claim an interest in what was featured in the comic books, but not over the original Conan character who had been delineated by Robert Howard in a series of stories in the 1930s. Howard's stories had passed into the public domain. CPI sued Mattel for its He-Man action figure, contending the action figure was too closely related to the visual representation of Conan in its comic books. Mattel defended He-Man by maintaining that CPI's character failed to meet the originality standard.

The court seemed troubled by the lack of creativity in CPI's Conan yet refused to actually find insufficient creativity. The judge admitted, "Just what, if anything, original CPI has contributed is difficult to discern." He noted that Conan in the comic books looked no different from a universe of hunky, superhero musclemen like Hercules, Tarzan, and John Carter, all of whom had the same square-jawed and broad-shouldered appeal. Yet rather than deeming the creativity requirement unsatisfied, he latched onto the comment, made by CPI's attorney during oral argument, that CPI's Conan "possesses a uniquely styled musculature, which differs significantly both from the other superhero hunks of the fantasy comic world, and from the lithe, swimmer-like Conan depicted in the illustrations that accompanied Howard's books."[11] Agreeing that "accentuat[ion] [of] certain muscle groups relative to others" can "constitute the protectable expression of an idea," the court found CPI to have satisfied the creativity threshold so that it could proceed in a battle over infringement with He-Man.

The court then moved on to the infringement analysis and a comparison of the two muscular heroes. The court found these works were not substantially similar and that "no reasonable trier of fact could conclude otherwise." But the only explanation it offered was tucked into a footnote. The footnote stated that CPI's Conan "is probably no better muscled than body-builder Arnold Schwarzenegger." It then explained that Schwarzenegger had a 57-inch chest and 20-inch calves when he won the Mr. Olympia title in 1977. Calculating that the He-Man doll, if enlarged to a height of six feet two inches, would boast a

71-inch chest and 29-inch calves, the judge concluded that this difference in musculature was enough for the two muscle men not to appear substantially similar to the ordinary observer.[12]

This infringement analysis leaves a lot to be desired. Although Schwarzenegger played Conan the Barbarian in two feature films, it is hard to know why he was the right template for evaluating the characteristics of the Conan character as illustrated in the comic books. Moreover, it seems unlikely that audiences would be able to appreciate the differences in muscle size the court deemed so critical given the small stature of the actual He-Man doll. A better approach would have been to determine from the beginning that there was nothing creative about the comic book Conan's musculature and decide the case on that basis, rather than rendering an opaque decision that offers no guidance to those looking to design the next swole action hero while avoiding an infringement claim from CPI.

Turning the creativity requirement into a rubber stamp exerts great pressure on the ill-defined tests for copyright infringement and fair use, making it harder for parties to predict the outcome of cases and artists to know in advance whether their behaviors run afoul of copyright law. When little attention is paid to eligibility questions, including creativity, the determination of a copyright's or design patent's proper scope in the infringement analysis becomes both more critical and more intricate. This can pose a particular problem for jurors, who are unfamiliar with copyright and patent law's concepts and competing aims.[13] Rather than adding more weight than the substantial similarity or fair use analyses can bear, it makes sense to structure the law in stages. A staged approach allows for striking various balances between rewarding creators and leaving enough raw material for downstream users. Studies show that strategically apportioning different analytical tasks in a lawsuit, instead of conflating them, helps curb tendencies to allow emotion or a desire to save cognitive energy to determine an outcome.[14]

A final concern with an ineffectual creativity screen is the potential for businesses to use their intellectual property rights to engage in nuisance lawsuits engineered to extract settlements and scare off competitors. This is particularly the case with design patents, which require ratification from the PTO. Even though the PTO greenlights most design patent applications, this seal of approval from a government agency carries some weight with federal courts, especially when no new prior art is introduced to challenge the PTO's nonobviousness determination.[15] As a result, notice of a design patent can dissuade downstream users seeking to borrow from even pedestrian, common-place designs. Even if they stand a good chance of winning on the issue of infringement, which admittedly requires a close match between the claimed design and the defendant's design, such users may conclude the risk and expense of litigation is not worth it.

In the end, the current ineffectual approach to creativity threatens the very purposes of copyright and design patent law. But the answer is not to abandon assessments of creativity altogether. Somewhat ironic-ally, the danger with an extremely generous creativity standard is that it may stifle creativity. The easier it is for authors or commercial design-ers to claim intellectual property protection, the harder it is for subse-quent creators to come up with their own non-infringing expressions. Awards of copyright or patent in uncreative material invite frivolous litigation from rightsholders, thereby deterring others who would otherwise engage in creative activity but do not want to get sued. This argues in favor of narrower construction of intellectual property entitlements. The rest of this chapter provides the operative principles for such a narrowing. Copyright's creativity requirement can be raised by considering artistic motivation and expert testimony. Through the teachings of the aesthetic middle, courts can identify which differences between designs are material and which are not. For both copyright and design patents, the art/science double standard should be replaced with rigorous comparisons to the prior art in the relevant creative domain.

FIXING COPYRIGHT'S CREATIVITY REQUIREMENT

In assessing creativity, courts hearing copyright cases make two par-ticular mistakes. They reject evidence of artistic motivation (or lack thereof), ignoring a much-needed source of content for the creativity analysis. They also ban the expert testimony necessary for an analysis sensitive to domain-specific differences. Given the neuroscientific lessons of the past two decades, it makes little sense for intellectual property law to continue to insist that the creative process has nothing to do with authorial mindsets or expert judgments.

Making Motivations Matter

By ignoring evidence of authorial motive, courts greatly expand the universe of copyrightable materials. Consider judicial treatment of photography. In the late nineteenth century, in a test case involving a staged photograph of the famed author Oscar Wilde, the US Supreme Court deemed the new technology of photography an appropriate subject for copyright protection. In doing so, the Court noted the various choices as to lighting, posing, etc. that were made by Wilde's photographer. By no means, however, did the Court imply that every click of the shutter should generate a copyrightable work. It explained that "an author who claims infringement must prove the existence of intellectual production, of thought, and conception," thereby suggesting only purposive activities should be eligible for copyright.[16]

Years later, a photographer's intentional choices became wholly irrelevant to the copyrightability of photographs. Judge Learned Hand speculated that all photographs enjoyed copyright protection, regardless of motive. "[N]o photograph, however simple, can be unaffected by the personal influence of the author, and no two will be absolutely alike," he explained.[17] Today, "[a]lmost any photograph 'may claim the necessary originality to support a copyright'."[18]

This generous posture toward photography depends on the exclusion of authorial narratives from the creativity analysis. Only on extremely rare occasions do courts find insufficient originality in a photograph. Instead, for the reasons given in Chapter 1, there has been resistance to using artistic motive to add substance to the creativity determination. Even the most thoughtful opinions about the proper scope of copyright in photography contend that the originality determination must focus only on the work itself and ignore the decisions that went into making that work.[19]

Blocked from examining authorial intent, courts in photography cases tend to find that a work's mere existence as a photograph qualifies the work as sufficiently original. Copyright scholar Eva

Subotnik describes this judicial reasoning as the "proxy of ontology," and it has produced some absurdity in copyright photography cases.[20] When a crested macaque named Naruto took a selfie with a camera left where the monkey could acquire it, a news agency asserted copyright in the photograph. An appellate court denied copyright in the photograph, but not for lack of creativity. Boxed in by decades of decisions pronouncing every photograph sufficiently creative, the court of appeals could not find that Naruto's accidental click of the shutter was uncreative. Instead, it was forced to rely on the different rationale that the copyright statute did not permit animals to be considered "authors."[21]

Photography is not the only art form where failure to consider intent contributes to the impotence of the creativity requirement. Various digital technologies afford amateurs the tools to take constant snapshots of their surroundings. With the touch of a button, our phones record audio and video at any place and any time. Easily accessible software allows anyone to produce computer-generated imagery. As we unthinkingly produce more and more content, copyright law prevents courts from using the heedless nature of that production to place a check on the expansion of copyright protection.

Taking evidence of motivation seriously will require the trier of fact to scrutinize narratives of artistic initiative and not simply accept a story of creative inspiration at face value. Although this kind of interrogation of rationales for human behavior occurs all the time in the courts, today, a copyright claimant can demand protection for their work without bothering to craft an explanation that suggests creative activity. As Subotnik writes about ways of assessing the creativity of photographs, "as between an assertion that 'if X is a photograph, then it is original,' and some compelling, or at least plausible explanation of what a photographer was trying to accomplish, the latter is more capable of being subject to scrutiny in litigation ... and therefore is a more justifiable basis for copyright protection."[22]

An additional argument in favor of considering evidence of creative motivation in the creativity assessment is that, to a very limited degree, it is already being done. As compared to the general approach in copyright cases, courts have been more willing to probe authorial motivations when the work at issue is a derivative work, i.e., one that is heavily based on another copyrightable work.[23] In these situations, when the derivative work must be analyzed to make sure it satisfies the requirements for originality and is sufficiently distinguishable from the preexisting work, courts sometimes look to authorial purpose. This isolated trend in some derivative works cases should become a formalized approach in all creativity evaluations.

L. Batlin & Son v. *Snyder*, a favorite of copyright casebooks, illustrates the approach sometimes taken. The case involved a claim of copyright in a plastic toy bank modeled after a metal toy bank in the public domain. A court of appeals held that the plastic bank was not original. The court deemed variations between the metal and plastic versions of the bank trivial, in part, because the plaintiff manufacturer made the changes for efficiency and cost reasons rather than out of some creative vision. Changes made only "in order to fit into the required price range and quantity and quality of material to be used" did not reflect a creative impulse so much as an attempt to appropriate public domain work.[24]

A few other derivative works cases take the same approach. In *Meshwerks, Inc.* v. *Toyota Motor Sales U.S.A., Inc.*, then court of appeals judge Neil Gorsuch assessed whether two-dimensional digital models of cars generated for an advertising campaign were deserving of copyright. In concluding that the models were not original, Gorsuch highlighted the designers' description of their modeling work "as an attempt accurately to depict real-world, three-dimensional objects as digital images viewable on a computer screen."[25] Along similar lines, a judge held photographic reproductions of works of art in the public domain uncopyrightable because the "point of the exercise" was "to reproduce the underlying works with absolute fidelity," which made them "nothing more than slavish copies."[26]

Cases like *Batlin* and *Meshwerks* have been criticized for employing their own, higher creativity standard. But it is not so much a different standard being applied as a different evidentiary rule. For good reason, cases involving the copyrightability of derivative works activate the fears of judges that the would-be author is a mere copyist. As a consequence, judges tend to reach into their bag of traditional legal tools and interrogate the parties' motives. This interrogation allows courts to assess creativity in a more searching manner than in the average case. Given what we now know about the centrality of author-ial intent to creative output, these tools should be deployed in all copyright cases where creativity is at issue, not just cases involving derivative works.

Embracing Expertise

Artistic domains differ. Some have more specific rules and more total rules than others.[27] In some areas, like jazz music or experimental arts, "vast degrees of newness are expected and acclaimed."[28] Psychologists tell us that to appreciate a domain-specific view of creative potential, we need the input of domain-specific experts. Yet rather than welcom-ing such information to help titrate the creativity standard to individual cases, courts have been inhospitable to expert evidence in the creativity determination.

This is where perhaps the *Bleistein* decision has had its greatest impact. *Bleistein* maintains that any evaluation of artistic creativity involves a special kind of judgment that even the most informed cannot agree upon. The cliché "beauty is in the eye of the beholder" controls discussion of aesthetic judgments in the law. Because courts assume all expert opinion on such matters is simply a question of personal taste, experts are blocked from informing judicial decision-making in a var-iety of aesthetic areas, including copyright law.

In reality, expert judgments about art involve much more than simply asking if someone enjoys an expressive work or thinks it has great value. Even if taste is relative, agreement can coalesce over such topics as what is the appropriate definition of a particular genre of visual art or what are the conventions of a specific musical domain. Research shows that those with expertise in a domain tend to inde-pendently agree on their assessment of the creativity of new works in that domain. Even if one thinks that a layperson's judgment of an artwork's beauty is a "subjective practice [that] would normally be anathema to the ideal of objective legal standards,"[29] elements of evaluation of aesthetic worth can submit to reasoned interrogation, particularly by those with experience and training in the domain.

The best proof of this comes from other areas of copyright law that already welcome expert testimony to determine the value of artistic work. Under the Visual Artists Rights Act (VARA), artists producing limited edition visual works can prevent destruction of those works by subsequent owners so long as the works are proved to be of "recognized stature."[30] As courts have defined what "recognized stature" must mean, they have promoted the role of art experts. In one influential formulation, proof of recognized stature requires the testimony of "art experts" or "other members of the artistic community."[31] Although some subsequent cases permit alternatives to expert testimony, most decisions on "recognized stature" highlight the central importance of expertise. Even in those cases not mandating expert testimony, "generally accepted standards of the artistic community" from other informational resources were applied to determine the work's stature.[32]

Expert testimony on creativity has also found its way into copyright's fair use defense. Courts routinely evaluate the level of creativity in a defendant's work to assess "transformativeness" for purposes of the defense.[33] A transformative use employs a work for a different purpose or in a different manner than the original.[34] On some occasions, expert testimony on the subject is taken, and some have called for more regularized use of experts to help inform this analysis.[35]

Experts can provide information on the surrounding works in the relevant artistic area, information that is essential to understanding creativity at the level of domain. Such information is regularly offered when it comes to evaluating scientific creativity under utility patent law's nonobviousness standard, but eschewed by copyright's creativity analysis out of a belief that artistic creativity lies beyond objective comprehension. We now know that artistic and scientific creation are much the same; neuroscience confirms that theories of left-brained, analytical inventors and right-brained, unsystematic artists are false. Ending the art/science double standard would allow courts to take into account relevant prior art for a more rigorous evaluation of creativity.

Some might object that greater emphasis on prior art to assess creativity unfairly taxes artists with knowledge of the previous works in their domain. This is a burden we expect inventors to shoulder in utility patent law, but ascertaining relevant prior art may be more difficult for artists. Unlike patented inventions, there is no comprehensive registry of copyrighted works for artists to consult. Advances in visual art, music, and literature are arguably less susceptible to index-ing than scientific and technological improvements.

Still, we now know that knowledge of a domain's prior works is essential to creative production. Experience with and training in the conventions of the domain are critical factors in the generation of work that can transcend those conventions. If the goal is to align the creativ-ity requirement with the realities of the creative process, greater atten-tion to prior art makes sense. Given that psychologists posit that the creative process demands domain-specific knowledge of what works have come before, we should be skeptical of arguments that authors cannot be charged with awareness of the prior art in their domain. In addition, existing proposals to make copyrighted works more search-able could be implemented so that it would be easier for authors to find relevant prior works.[36]

A final concern relates to the cost to copyright litigants when hiring those with expertise in a creative domain. It is true that expert testi-mony can be expensive and one should be wary of reforms to the creativity requirement that threaten to price out deserving authors from vindicating their rights in court. Such testimony will not be required in every case, however. In some situations, it will be obvious that the plaintiff has reached even a more than minimal creativity threshold and the parties will stipulate.[37] Judges will need less help tracing the contours of some artistic domains than others. Like every-one else in the early 1990s, the nine justices hearing the *Feist* case were familiar with phone directories and could confidently assert that alpha-betical ordering of names was not only typical but uniform for that product. Judges may be already aware of the relevant conventions in literary works, but lacking in such knowledge when it comes to pho-tography or appropriation art.

Other areas of the law manage to accommodate expert testimony on a regular basis despite its expense. In utility patent law, courts have standardized the use of experts in claim-construction hearings so they can understand the claims from the perspective of "one of ordinary skill in the art." Something similar in copyright law could be used to allow judges and juries to learn the boundaries and benchmarks of the relevant artistic community. Without experts, judges and jurors are left to their own intuitions about what seems creative and what does not.

Instead of avoiding information central to understanding the creative process, it makes sense to encourage parties to build a record illustrating the conventions and shared practices of the relevant domain.

CALIBRATING NONOBVIOUSNESS TO DESIGN INNOVATION

For some creative territories, even with the benefit of expert input, it may be difficult to find agreed upon standards and benchmarks for evaluating artistic output. At least temporarily, when such information is lacking, it may be necessary to maintain a generous creativity evaluation. For commercial design, however, information germane to making an informed decision about a design's creativity exists, thanks to the academic and private researchers studying consumer decision-making. Their study of the aesthetic middle offers specific criteria that can be used to determine if a design represents an innovative break from the past. A difference from the prior art that tilts away from the aesthetic middle by making the design harder to process should be considered relevant to the nonobviousness determination; a difference from the prior art that increases a design's perceptual, repetition, or conceptual fluency should not. Such an approach would improve the current overly generous approach to design patent protection, which does nothing to encourage avant-garde commercial design.

Innovation Over Pleasure

Two particular qualities have been highlighted by the courts in construing design nonobviousness: innovation and pleasure. One strand of legal authority focuses on the designer and contends that a patentable design must demonstrate "a creative skill surpassing that of the routine."[38] Another trains its attention on consumers and posits that design patents should be reserved for commercial designs that are "beautiful, appealing to the eye, and causing a buying demand for the design."[39] Often courts mention both qualities in the same breath, implicitly assuming that ordinary observers naturally hold an aesthetic preference for innovative designs. We now know that this assumption is false, that aesthetic preference in design, rather than rewarding inventiveness, favors simplicity, familiarity, and congruence with the relevant product category. This means that construing the nonobviousness requirement in terms of audience pleasure will not promote design innovation.

One could accept that there is a disconnect between innovation and aesthetic preference, but contend that design patent law should only be geared to the production of pleasing, if not necessarily pioneering, designs. Citing beautification and public enjoyment as goals of design patent law only tells us so much about the standards that should be set for nonobviousness, however. If the success of design patent law is measured by maximizing the amount of beautiful design in society, it is unclear that the current generous approach to nonobviousness has been successful. There is no evidence that there is more beauty in our current commercial surroundings than there was before the Federal Circuit watered down the nonobviousness analysis. And even if we could somehow quantify an appreciable increase in the aesthetic quality of those surroundings, there is no evidence that the increase should be attributed to design patent protection. Overly generous intellectual property protections can sometimes stifle the very activity they are trying to encourage. Years ago, a federal judge aptly described the dilemma: "Overprotecting intellectual property is as harmful as underprotecting it. Creativity is impossible without a rich public domain. Nothing today, likely nothing since we tamed fire, is genuinely new: Culture, like science and technology, grows by accretion, each new creator building on the works of those who came before. Overprotection stifles the very creative forces it's supposed to nurture."[40]

The design patent battle between Apple and Samsung offers an illustrative example. Design patent law lacks the constraints of other intellectual property regimes when it comes to preserving space for competition. This means that recognition of a design patent in simplistic yet desirable aesthetic features gives the patent holder latitude to charge exorbitant rents and insulate itself from price competition. If people inherently like their phones flat and minimalist, cases like *Apple* make it less likely that competitors will be able to offer such phones at a reduced price. Even design patents that are never enforced can still have the effect of inhibiting competition in similar styles. Perhaps it is no coincidence that Apple's smartphones and tablets cost more than other smartphones and tablets. The availability of patent protection for design features that audiences find most aesthetically preferable – i.e., features in the aesthetic middle – raises the price of pleasing design for consumers.

Even if we conclude that the nonobviousness requirement should be geared to design innovation, rather than audience pleasure, there is still the question of how to assess innovation. This is where neuroscientific study of aesthetic preference comes in. The nonobviousness requirement can be bolstered by protecting only those design choices that detract from processing fluency – i.e., those that are less aesthetically preferred. Such a reform would reserve the incentive of design patent protection for the designers that need it most. The slow public embrace of Herman Miller's pioneering Aeron chair is a telling example. To recoup their investment in a particular design, innovative designers need time for the design to incubate with the public. Absent the security of a patent, Herman Miller may have viewed a multi-year campaign to change public perception as economically unsound and elected to never produce the Aeron chair.

Without some way to protect their investment while keeping it in the public eye, such designers will be dissuaded from launching pioneering products, even if they believe such products will eventually enjoy mass appeal. In these situations, the anti-competitive costs of design patent enforcement may be warranted. But designs possessing conventionally pleasing visual features do not warrant patent protection – because they display no inventiveness and they can enjoy some immediate favor in the marketplace, they have less need of a legal incentive. In this way, aesthetic preference can be made relevant to design patent law, but not in the manner it is currently instantiated in nonobviousness doctrine.

Of course, it is difficult to craft a law perfectly aligned with all of the real-world influences involved in the creation and production of commercial products. Many things can factor into a business's decision to bring a particular design to market. Ease of manufacture, the designer's personal aesthetic, or other considerations may shape this decision. Nevertheless, known sources of consumer demand must be of overriding importance when it comes to assessing the incentive structure for commercial design. Industrial designers are already aware of the principles of the aesthetic middle and processing fluency and act accordingly. Correlating nonobviousness to design choices that run counter to those principles reserves the incentive of patent protection for where it is most needed. The next section illustrates how the teachings of the aesthetic middle can be operationalized to determine when a new design sufficiently departs from the designs that came before it.

Identifying Material Design Differences

If design patent law is supposed to spur design innovation, it is time to abandon the primary reference requirement. Under the requirement, any minor difference is sufficient for patentability even if multiple items in the prior art can be combined to recreate the exact design at issue. Such a cramped analysis of the prior art encourages designers to make only the most minimal departures from what came before. By taking such a narrow view of relevant prior art for the nonobviousness determination, today's design patent law rewards designs in the aesthetic middle that likely would already be produced without the added attraction of a fifteen-year competitive blockade. Abandoning the primary reference rule and considering a greater array of prior art would boost the nonobviousness standard in a way that rewards only designs with innovative features, not ones that merely repeat conventional choices.

Even with more prior art to consider for the nonobviousness determination, there still remains the difficult issue of determining when a difference from the prior art should render a design nonobvious. The current test insists that design appreciation is holistic and any difference determinative. Instead of upgrading or downgrading a difference according to its real effect on consumers, almost any variance between the claimed design and the prior art, regardless of its actual relevance, is enough. For example, even when possessing the very same features as the prior art, claimed designs can sufficiently distinguish themselves from the prior art by simply exhibiting more contrast between those features.[41] Any difference is material, even a design choice that makes the item look more conventional or simplistic. In a case involving home furniture, just replacing an existing design's more ornate veneer with a plain one was enough to satisfy nonobviousness.[42]

By analyzing the effect of a design choice on processing fluency, courts can stop treating all design differences the same. Take, for example, a situation involving two similar designs that differ only as to a single design choice that enhances rather than detracts from perceptual fluency, i.e., fluency stemming from an object's overall simplicity. A Federal Circuit case from the early 1990s, decided before the nonobviousness test had been rendered a non-entity, is illustrative. The case involved a claimed design for a bottle with two compartments. There were other dual-compartment bottles in the prior art, but the patentee contended that its bottle was nonobvious because it was "symmetrical around a plane vertically bisecting the bottle" whereas pre-existing designs did not "teach a symmetrical design." Although it was true that the prior art did not exhibit the same symmetricality as the claimed design, the court correctly concluded that this was an immaterial difference. Symmetry is a well-known design strategy for increasing aesthetic preference. The court explained that designers are quite aware of the potential for making features in a design symmetrical; in fact "the *expected* design configuration is one of symmetry."[43]

A material design difference relating to perceptual fluency would be one that requires more cognitive resources to process. Hence, a design choice away from symmetry should be presumed a material difference. So should a choice to reduce the contrast between design features. Although not framed in terms of perceptual fluency, in the *Apple* case, the Federal Circuit noted that the screens in older tablet computers stood out as opposed to the sleeker iPad design, which deemphasized the contrast between its screen and the rest of the device.[44] This is actually a difference worth noting for nonobviousness as less contrast in the iPad design translates to less perceptual fluency.

In addition to perceptual fluency, repetition fluency and conceptual fluency can also be used to determine relevant differences between a design and the prior art. The current nonobviousness analysis does little to encourage departures from everyday prototypical forms. A six-sided cardboard box can defeat a charge of obviousness, at least on summary judgment, even though the claimed aspects of a solid bottom and flaps that fit into slots are so common in various packaging forms as to be almost unnoticeable.[45] Design patents routinely issue for common geometric shapes, as for the user interface shown in Figure 6.1, which displays nothing more than three rectangles with a square beneath.[46] Our natural inclination to the aesthetic middle means that familiar, prototypical designs are aesthetically favored whereas designs that are unfamiliar receive lower aesthetic rankings. This means that a design difference from the prior art that moves away from familiar forms should be considered more relevant to nonobviousness than a design choice that hews to common prototypes.

Again, an older case, decided before liberalization of the nonobviousness standard, illustrates how design differences can be evaluated with an eye to repetition fluency. By designing a telephone with a mouthpiece mounted on a column and a receiver suspended from a hook on the column, a business tried to appeal to consumer nostalgia for the old-fashioned upright telephones of the early twentieth century (Figure 6.2). The PTO granted the business's application for a design patent,[47] but a competitor challenged the design patent on the phone as obvious.

Agreeing with the competitor, the court in review emphasized the designer's goal of invoking familiar phone prototypes. Although there were some differences between the design and the prior art, the "overall visual impression" was too similar to what had come before to be nonobvious.[48] The court cautioned that merely trying for a "nostalgic effect" should not automatically render a design obvious.[49] But the designer's clear effort to remind observers of the category of old phones made the court rightfully skeptical that the designer had sufficiently distinguished its phone from the prior art.

While design choices reflecting the familiar should be given little weight, design choices that reduce repetition fluency should be considered material. Though more common now, Corelle's hook-handle coffee cup design (see Figure 6.3) departed from the other familiar coffee cup prototypes of the time in that its ring handle was not attached at both ends to the cup.[50] Such a design choice to depart from the familiar should be considered material as it makes the design more difficult for the consumer to initially decode.

Along the same lines, a design choice that lends itself to conceptual fluency should be considered presumptively obvious whereas a design

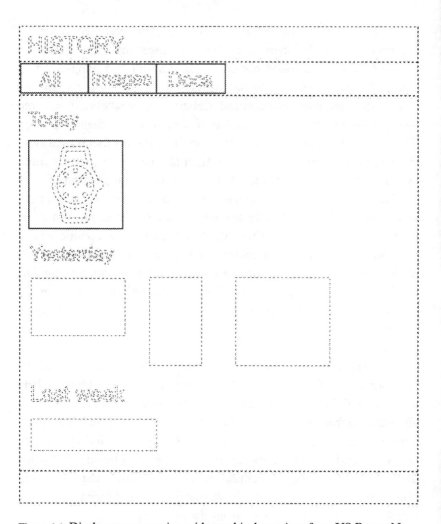

Figure 6.1 Display screen portion with graphical user interface, US Patent No. D767,583 (Sept. 27, 2016). The broken-lined figures are not part of the claimed design.

that is incongruent with the product category decreases conceptual fluency and, hence, should be more likely to be considered nonobvious. Take the real case of a motorcycle break lever in the shape of a naked human female body (Figure 6.4).[51]

This design lacks conceptual fluency in that it confounds expectations for the category of motorcycle levers. Nothing about the form is

Figure 6.2 Desk telephone, US Patent No. D224,911 (Oct. 10, 1972).

Figure 6.3 Corelle Old Town Blue hook handle cups. Image courtesy of the Corning Incorporated Department of Archives and Records Management, Corning, NY.

a clue to the utilitarian item being sold. Seeing the female form as a motorcycle lever forces the observer to think harder than in a situation where the lever is represented in a form one is more likely to associate with motorcycles. A case involving a design for a doll utilizing a human form would be different. In that situation, the design has strong conceptual fluency as it aligns with the product being sold and a court should be more inclined to a finding of obviousness.

Figure 6.4 Motorcycle brake or clutch lever, US Patent No. D432,470 (Oct. 24, 2000).

The current nonobviousness analysis does not take into account a design's conceptual fluency. Take the example of toy titan Lego. Lego holds several copyrights on the visual appearance of its toys. In recent years, it has also sought additional protection by securing design patents on the same items, including the one depicted in Figure 6.5.

When the design was challenged as obvious by a rival toymaker in 2019, the same court that rightly found the old-fashioned telephone obvious years before quickly declared the Lego brick nonobvious and patentable. The court relied on the description of Lego's expert, who characterized the patent as follows:

> a sort of a really lovely, balanced form. So I'm talking about the proportion. So the length and width in proportion to all the other sides. It's kind of unique in that the top slab is slightly thicker than

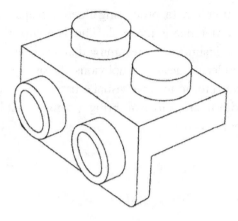

Figure 6.5 Building block from a toy building set, US Patent No. D688,328S (Aug. 20, 2013).

the front. I'm calling this the front. So the top is thicker. So that can imply a lot of different uses. It feels really open to be used in any direction, horizontal, vertical. And because there are two – these two stud projections, feels like they can become very decorative in their use as well.[52]

For another similar Lego design patent, the court deemed it significant that the same expert described the block as an "open-ended form" and "cute."[53]

A design that is "open-ended" or that can "imply a lot of different uses" does nothing to challenge an observer's conceptual fluency. This is an example of an expert (and a court relying on the expert) seizing on any difference with the prior art as opposed to diagnosing differences that matter. A better course would be to examine whether the design implicates a different category from the proffered product. It is hard to see how this particular design does. Particularly when the functional aspects of the connecting studs are removed from the comparison with the prior art, the Lego design appears like many typical forms, both in general and in the category of toy building blocks, even if some minor differences may exist. Consideration of conceptual fluency offers a means for denying protection for designs that do nothing more than incorporate simple geometric forms, reserving the rewards of patent protection for designs that depart from the tried and true.[54]

In general, attention to processing fluency helps the trier of fact decide when a difference is material. This is a superior approach to merely relying on instinct and presuming that any difference from what came before renders a design nonobvious. Design patent protection should be a reward for innovative visual artistry, not an entitlement for any business with the resources to bring a commercial item to market and hire a patent attorney.

Notes

1   Dennis S. Karjala, *Copyright and Creativity*, 15 UCLA Ent. L. Rev. 169, 201 (2008).

2   Brian L. Frye, *Against Creativity*, 11 N.Y.U. J. L. & Liberty 426, 428 (2017). See also Aaron X. Fellmeth, *Uncreative Intellectual Property Law*, 27 Tex. Intell. Prop. L.J. 51, 86 (2019) ("[T]he goal of copyright law is ... securing a sufficient quantity of expressive works for the public benefit, with no very significant interest in the quality of the resulting works.").

3   Jeanne C. Fromer, *A Psychology of Intellectual Property*, 104 Nw. U. L. Rev. 1441, 1498 (2010). For scientific creations, Fromer found that the public is conditioned to evaluate works according to improvements from past baselines and to treasure significant departures from past learning, thus validating utility patent law's contrasting objective approach to evaluating creativity under the nonobviousness standard.

4   U.S. Const. art. I, § 8, cl. 8.

5   Leslee Lazar, *The Cognitive Neuroscience of Design Creativity*, 12 J. Exp. Neurosci. 1, 1–3 (2018); Vera Makern et al., *Computations Models of Creativity: A Review of Single-Process and Multi-Process Recent Approaches to Demystify Creative Cognition*, 27 Current Op. Behav. Sci. 47, 47 (2019).

6   See Orit Fischman Afori, *Reconceptualizing Property in Designs*, 25 Cardozo Arts & Entmt. L.J. 1105, 1135–41 (2008).

7   Mark A. Lemley & Mark P. McKenna, *Scope*, 57 Wm. & Mary L. Rev. 2197, 2209 (2016).

8   Cambridge University Press v. Patton, 769 F.3d 1232, 1268 (11th Cir. 2014).

9   Design patent law has no fair use defense, making the initial validity determination (and any determination of infringement) even more critical to the overall outcome of the case.

10   712 F. Supp. 353 (S.D.N.Y. 1989).

11   *Id.*

12   *Id.* at 361 n.14.

13   Lemley & McKenna, *supra*, at 2219.

[14] See Chris Guthrie et. al., *Blinking on the Bench: How Judges Decide Cases*, 93 CORNELL L. REV. 1, 41 (2007); Joep Sonnemans & Frans Van Dijk, *Errors in Judicial Decisions: Experimental Results*, 28 J. L. ECON. & ORG. 687, 714 (2011).

[15] PowerOasis, Inc. v. T-Mobile USA, Inc., 522 F.3d 1299, 1304 (Fed. Cir. 2008).

[16] Burrow-Giles Lithographic Co. v. Sarony, 111 U.S. 53, 59–60 (1884).

[17] Jewelers' Circular Pub. Co. v. Keystone Pub. Co., 274 F. 932, 934–35 (S.D.N.Y. 1921). See also SHL Imaging, Inc. v. Artisan House, Inc., 117 F. Supp. 2d 301, 310 (S.D.N.Y. 2000) ("The technical aspects of photography imbue the medium with almost limitless creative potential.").

[18] Mannion v. Coors Brewing Co., 377 F. Supp. 2d 444, 450 (S.D.N.Y. 2005) (quoting MELVILLE B. NIMMER & DAVID NIMMER, 1 NIMMER ON COPYRIGHT § 2.08 [E][1]).

[19] *Id.* at 451.

[20] Eva E. Subotnik, *Originality Proxies: Toward a Theory of Copyright and Creativity*, 76 BROOK. L. REV. 1487, 1513–14 (2011).

[21] Naruto v. Slater, 888 F.3d 418, 425–26 (9th Cir. 2018).

[22] Subotnik, *supra*, at 1531.

[23] The Copyright Act defines "derivative work" as "a work based upon one or more preexisting works." 17 U.S.C. § 101.

[24] L. Batlin & Son, Inc. v. Snyder, 536 F.2d 486, 487–89 (2d Cir. 1976).

[25] 528 F.3d 1258, 1269 (10th Cir. 2008).

[26] Bridgeman Art Library, Ltd. v. Corel Corp., 36 F. Supp. 2d 191, 197 (S.D.N.Y. 1999).

[27] MIHALY CSIKSZENTMIHALYI, CREATIVITY: FLOW AND THE PSYCHOLOGY OF DISCOVERY AND INVENTION 38–40 (1996).

[28] Fromer, *supra*, at 1507.

[29] Andrew W. Torrance, *Beauty Fades: An Experimental Study of Federal Court Design Patent Aesthetics*, 19 J. INTELL. PROP. L. 389, 390 (2012).

[30] 17 U.S.C. § 106A.

[31] Carter v. Helmsley-Spear, Inc., 861 F. Supp. 303, 325 (S.D.N.Y. 1994).

[32] See Cohen v. G & M Realty L.P., 320 F. Supp. 3d 421, 438 (E.D.N.Y. 2018).

[33] Shyamkrishna Balganesh, *Tiered Originality and the Dualism of Copyright Incentives*, 95 VA. L. REV. IN BRIEF 67, 73 (2009).

[34] Bouchat v. Baltimore Ravens Ltd. P'ship, 619 F.3d 301, 308 (4th Cir. 2010).

[35] Holly Gordon, *Appropriation Artists and Testifying Experts: Reconciling Postmodern Artistic Expression and Copyright Law*, 43 AIPLA Q.J. 445, 485–87 (2015); Monika Isia Jasiewicz, *"A Dangerous Undertaking": The Problem of Intentionalism and Promise of Expert Testimony*, 26 YALE J. L. & HUMAN. 143, 171 (2014).

36 See Jeanne C. Fromer, *Claiming Intellectual Property,* 76 U. CHI. L. REV. 719, 781–94 (2009).

37 See, for example, Dr. Seuss Enterprises, L.P. v. ComicMix LLC, 372 F. Supp. 3d 1101, 1116 (S.D. Cal. 2019).

38 Lancaster Colony Corp. v. Aldon Accessories, 506 F.2d 1197, 1199 (2d Cir. 1974).

39 J.R. Wood & Sons, Inc. v. Abelson's, Inc., 74 F.2d 895 (3d Cir. 1934).

40 White v. Samsung Elecs. Am., Inc., 989 F.2d 1512, 1513 (9th Cir. 1993) (Kozinski, J., dissenting).

41 Sealy Tech. v. SSB Mfg. Co., 825 Fed. Appx. 795 (Fed. Cir. 2020).

42 Ashley Furniture Indus., Inc. v. Lifestyle Enter., Inc., 574 F. Supp. 2d 920, 933 (W.D. Wisc. 2008).

43 *In re* Carlson, 983 F.2d 1032, 1038–39 (Fed. Cir. 1993).

44 Apple, Inc. v. Samsung Elecs. Co., 678 F.3d 1314, 1331–32 (Fed. Cir. 2012).

45 Poly-America v. API Industries, Inc., 74 F. Supp. 3d 685, 690, 697 (D. Del. 2014).

46 U.S. Patent No. D767,583 (Sept. 27, 2016).

47 U.S. Patent No. D224,911 (Oct. 10, 1972).

48 United States Tel. Co. v. American Telecomm. Corp., 204 U.S.P.Q. 951, at *1, *6–*8 (D. Conn. 1979).

49 *Id.* at *7.

50 Corelle Old Town Blue hook handle cups. Image courtesy of the Corning Incorporated Department of Archives and Records Management, Corning, NY.

51 Durdin v. Kuryakyn Holdings, Inc., 440 F. Supp. 2d 921 (W.D. Wisc. 2006).

52 Lego A/S v. Zuru, Inc., 2019 WL 4643718, *12–*14 (D. Conn., July 8, 2019).

53 *Id.* at *12.

54 This is not to say that every design that avoids confusing consumers as to its relevant product category should be considered obvious. Such an approach would be an overcorrection to the permissiveness of the current nonobviousness test. But conceptual fluency should be one consideration among others in evaluating whether a design's departure from the prior art is sufficient. There may be situations where a design is challenging when it comes to one type of processing fluency but the design reinforces the teachings of the aesthetic middle for other types of processing fluency.

7 KNOW YOUR AUDIENCE

Creativity and nonobviousness are not the only legal tests that can benefit from the greater specificity afforded by neuroscientific discoveries. The current substantial similarity analysis asks judges and juries to divine the aesthetic judgment of audiences to determine whether one work infringes the copyright of another. Copyright law deems aesthetic judgment inherently subjective and, therefore, not susceptible to measurement or the imposition of objective criteria, yet also universal, making attention to audience differences largely unnecessary. By offering empirical evidence of audience reaction, neuroaesthetic research refutes these judicial theories about art appreciation. It turns out that we can measure aesthetic experiences and that these experiences vary depending on audience and artistic medium.

Before rushing to use neuroaesthetic research to change copyright law's view of audiences, however, we should first ask some fundamental questions. Just because aesthetic response can now be measured that does not mean that such measurements should guide the infringement determination. There are reasons to be wary of using scientific measurement of audience behavior to change the law of copyright infringement. Some embrace copyright law's current focus on aesthetic reactions but worry that privileging neuroscientific measurements of those responses would do violence to the humanistic values embedded in copyright law. A contrasting position would rather aesthetic considerations be purged from the infringement calculus altogether. Adoption of either viewpoint would have the same effect: stopping neuroscience's influence on copyright infringement before it can get started. I address both concerns before turning to some specific and realizable recommendations for bringing neuroaesthetic insights into the substantial similarity analysis.

153

SAFEGUARDING AESTHETIC PLURALISM

At its heart, neuroaesthetics forces a partial reconception of our experience of creative works, painting this experience as a matter of biology. This shift can be jarring for its implied displacement of longstanding cultural considerations. Perhaps some injection of empirical assessment into aesthetics can be tolerated, but, if too concerned with finding objective answers, neuroscientists may create those answers even if they do not truly describe what makes art pleasurable to audiences. It does not help that the things being studied – "beauty," "pleasure," "similarity" – lack universally accepted definitions. The vague, undefined nature of aesthetic experience, it is feared, will give scientists too much leverage to impose their own definitions. As one philosopher wrote with regard to psychological studies of art appreciation, "I am convinced that the problem of the description of the nature of aesthetic experience is not a task to which the techniques of empirical science are relevant."[1] Anxious art historians and critics complain that neuroscientists rarely consult their work when charting new discoveries in aesthetic science.[2]

A related note of critique when it comes to neuroaesthetics stems from the tendency of neuroscientists to study "classic" artistic representations, thereby embedding in a supposedly objective analysis of aesthetic experience their own tastes and predispositions. Many neuroaesthetic experiments expose subjects to paintings and sculptures in what would now be considered traditional styles. At the same time, by searching for the biological signs of aesthetic beauty and pleasure, neuroscientists can be accused of reifying outdated aesthetic theories. For example, one art critic accuses neuroscientists of using their enhanced ability to study viewer sensations to only chase an old-fashioned view of art as dependent on a work's formal properties. Better to investigate the work's meaning, and related social and historical backdrop, he says, which cannot be elucidated so easily through neural imaging. Otherwise, the scientists conducting neural studies of audiences will impose their own artistic tastes on copyright law, giving short shrift to conceptual art or other artistic movements that do not square with an old, Enlightenment view of aesthetics.[3]

It seems wrong, however, to insist that our understanding of aesthetic experiences cannot be improved by new knowledge of neural architectures. Neuroscientists need to be careful about instantiating eighteenth-century theories of aesthetics into experiments meant to track how twenty-first century audiences perceive creative works. Studies involving only classical works of art will of course privilege certain art forms over others. But researchers are increasingly evaluating different kinds of art, including conceptual art.[4] In its earliest stages, it made sense for neuroaesthetic study to focus on works of art that enjoyed the most popular acclaim, thereby minimizing individual variance when it comes to perceiving a work as "beautiful." This prompted a reliance on more traditional works. But it seems likely that a broader description of the different inputs for aesthetic experience will come as the body of scientific studies grows.

Nor is it impossible to conceive of a role for neuroaesthetic data that does not completely replace past understandings and measures of our aesthetic encounters. Such data, rather than supplanting the reported aesthetic reactions of observers and listeners, can act as a valuable supplement to articulated notions of beauty, pleasure, and similarity. Part of the value of neuroaesthetic study is that it can supply evidence of mental processes that individuals cannot perceive or describe on their own. Yet the goal is not to jettison conscious explorations of aesthetic encounters. Scientists check fMRI data derived from experiments on brain function against "reliable first-person accounts of consciousness," rather than replace reported descriptions of aesthetic experience altogether.[5] Objective evidence of audience reactions can be incorporated into the substantial similarity analysis without completely redefining or determining that analysis.

A related concern comes from the danger outside evidence of audience reaction poses to aesthetic pluralism. Although the overwhelming scholarly consensus is that the substantial similarity test needs more definition, for some, this lack of specificity should be considered a feature, not a bug. The undetermined nature of the test affords the trier of fact the opportunity to consider more than the economic effects of the appropriation, allowing for "the introduction and instantiation of pluralistic values into the copyright analysis."[6] The First Amendment commands aesthetic neutrality. If the vagueness of the current substantial similarity test aids this commitment to aesthetic pluralism, a more structured test, responsive to biological evidence of audience reaction, might potentially do the opposite.

Aesthetic pluralism is a worthwhile consideration in structuring the substantial similarity test, but some tension between the need for greater specificity in the definition of infringement and the desire to protect aesthetic pluralism is inevitable. Copyright policymakers need to weigh the costs and benefits of one approach against another rather than valuing pluralism over all other values. The years of frustration voiced by copyright scholars and judges over the substantial similarity test testifies to a consensus that the law has moved too far along the spectrum toward plurality and away from predictability. Lack of specifics as to what constitutes infringement makes copyright cases notoriously expensive as even somewhat specious claims become incapable of resolution before trial. Predictability is not the only value at stake in copyright jurisprudence, but it should be a central one.

The infringement test's unbounded nature allows for bias. In its present form, the test is not only unpredictable but permits wide disparities in the success rates of infringement suits depending on artistic medium. Plaintiffs claiming infringement of a musical composition fare far better than those alleging improper appropriation of a literary copyright.[7] There may be good reasons for some of this discrepancy, but the problem with the current state of infringement law is that we have no way of finding out why the discrepancy exists. The infringement black box makes it impossible to discern potential failures in judgment. Perhaps the variance in infringement decisions reflects a desirable ecumenical approach to art appreciation. But it also likely stems from decision-making errors, as when a jury bases its decision on unprotectable attributes of the plaintiff's work or on a retributive impulse after learning the defendant engaged in some intentional copying.[8]

Given these considerations, some potential sacrifice of aesthetic pluralism in favor of a more determined substantial similarity analysis is desirable. In addition, the specific reforms prompted by neuroaesthetic findings can be designed to do as little harm to pluralist values as possible. For example, one suggestion, described in more detail below, is to alter the infringement analysis to take into account the ways in which aesthetic encounters differ depending on the kind of work at issue. By incorporating neuroaesthetic discoveries into the law of substantial similarity, copyright reformers can make infringement more determined while at the same time avoiding a uniform approach to aesthetic judgment.

AVOIDING AESTHETICS

Inattention to aesthetic concerns would seem to follow Justice Holmes's admonition in *Bleistein* that judges should avoid making any sort of qualitative judgment when assessing whether a work is sufficiently original to warrant copyright protection. *Bleistein*'s influence on the specific issue of copyright infringement has been more muted than its influence on the creativity determination, but only because of the presumed impossibility of measuring audience reactions. By assuming that an audience's aesthetic judgment was impenetrable, courts were able to believe the substantial similarity analysis avoided the imposition of any aesthetic orthodoxy. After all, if one could not discern how jurors arrived at their infringement determinations, then arguably one could not steer those determinations in any particular direction. Longstanding prohibitions on expert testimony and audience survey evidence served as additional safeguards against influences that might violate *Bleistein*'s aesthetic non-discrimination principle when evaluating substantial similarity.

Decisions about the relevance of scientific evidence of aesthetic response tread much closer to an explicit qualitative judgment about art. Judicial choices about the probativity of such evidence would require decisions about how to prioritize findings that audiences find particular aspects of a work to be "beautiful" or just "noise." Rather than revising the substantial similarity test to incorporate this evidence and risk offending *Bleistein*, one might be tempted to jettison aesthetic concerns altogether. Such an anti-aesthetic approach would render neuroaesthetics of no value for copyright law.

There are a few reasons not to excise aesthetic concerns from copyright infringement, however. First, it may be impossible. As multiple scholars point out, judges frequently disclaim aesthetic principles in copyright cases while in fact relying on their own aesthetic sympathies to decide cases.[9] By maintaining that judges should not evaluate aesthetic merit, the *Bleistein* decision effectively adopts its own aesthetic theory, one that assesses aesthetic worth based on a work's market value. Considering evidence of aesthetic reaction would at least make judicial sympathies more transparent.

Second, an expressly non-aesthetic approach would likely substitute financial concerns for aesthetic ones. Some copyright scholars call for explicitly tethering commercial value to the infringement calculation. In 2010, a group proposed to change substantial similarity to "require the copyright owner to prove commercial harm in order to prove infringement of the owner's exclusive rights."[10] They maintained that this doctrinal reform would replace the audience test's subjectivity with an objective way to ascertain when appropriation of a creative work is improper.

We should question whether an infringement determination based solely on market harm, and no longer reliant on aesthetic reaction, would make sense. To the extent copyright law is designed to preserve financial incentives for authors, it is likely that other components of copyright doctrine are already doing the job. The toothless nature of the creativity requirement means that eligibility for copyright protection depends more on a work's potential marketability than its creativity. Copyright's fair use defense also relies heavily on economic harm. In evaluating the defense, courts must consider four statutory factors, including "the effect of the use upon the potential market for or value of the copyrighted work."[11] The Supreme Court described this factor as the "single most important element in determining fair use,"[12] and even as subsequent decisions have caused the fair use determination to evolve, federal courts continue to consider market harm to be of primary importance.[13]

Legal tests meant to emphasize financial considerations can have adverse consequences. For many, copyright law has become an engine for inequality. Tethering copyright protection to market value has produced a star system where the biggest entertainment companies and the most well-known celebrities gain the most from the law.[14] Yoking infringement exclusively to market value could have its own pernicious effects. It could fuel an unthinking "if value, then right" tendency in intellectual property law, enlarging the scope of copyright without considering competing values like the need for a robust public domain to provide raw material for new works of authorship.[15]

To address these concerns, there needs to be a mechanism for engaging non-economic values in the copyright infringement analysis. As copyright scholar Andrew Gilden persuasively argues, copyright decisions involving issues of copyrightability and fair use often employ economic rhetoric to justify the clandestine upholding of noneconomic interests such as sexual privacy, religious freedom, and democratic discourse.[16] Gilden objects to the use of "market gibberish" to obfuscate the real values that are being vindicated in these cases. The substantial similarity test potentially serves as a mechanism for supporting and articulating these values. But, in its current incarnation, there is not even "gibberish" to rely on to determine what is going on.

The answer is not to abandon aesthetic analysis altogether. If the subject matter of copyright protection makes such analysis unavoidable, then copyright law should change to make its selection of aesthetic principles open and notorious. As Gilden writes, "[i]f courts are going to engage in a deeply subjective endeavor, influenced by a wide variety of considerations, those considerations should be at least allowed to come to the surface."[17] Aesthetic reactions can serve as a proxy for additional values beyond preserving the financial incentives of authors. Neurological measurement has the potential to make these values more legible and prevent courts from hiding behind an outdated, mystical view of aesthetic experience.

THE RIGHT WAY TO INCORPORATE NEUROSCIENCE INTO COPYRIGHT LAW

Below I offer some suggestions for how neuroaesthetic findings can improve copyright infringement decision-making, using the lessons of neuroaesthetics to justify doctrinal reforms. Given the inertia of copyright lawmaking, they may not be realized immediately. Nevertheless, such reforms become increasingly likely as neuroaesthetics matures as a research field and courts grow more dissatisfied with the flawed state of the substantial similarity status quo.

Surveying Audience Difference

Neuroaesthetics demonstrates that copyright law's general assumption of audience universality is wrong. Gender, familiarity with a particular art form, and other factors impact perception of creative works. Because there is more variability in audiences than the law has assumed, there needs to be further guidance from courts to allow the trier of fact to adopt the perspective of intended audience members. Neuroscience lacks sufficient reliability to determine individual cases, but its larger discoveries about aesthetic judgment show the need for a more tailored inquiry into audience reaction. Survey evidence, long banned from the substantial similarity analysis, should be admitted to help judges and jurors understand different audiences in copyright cases just as it already is in trademark disputes.

By prompting greater attention to the reactions of intended audiences, surveys would alter the infringement analysis to better track the financial and non-financial harms of infringement. To the extent that the substantial similarity test is meant to assess economic harm from the defendant's copying, the reactions of people who will actually encounter the works provides a better sense of this harm than the reactions of the general public or individual triers of fact. Non-financial interests are also better represented by intended audience members. It is a desire to be known to a particular audience and to cultivate a favorable reputation among that audience, not just a desire for financial remuneration, that motivates artists.[18] It therefore makes sense to calibrate infringement according to the reactions of specific audiences for the plaintiff's and defendant's works.

Surveys also offer the capability of assessing audience reactions in a rapid manner that resembles the spontaneous and immediate aesthetic experiences of audience members in the real world. The limitations of the courtroom and the adversarial process make it difficult to determine the gut reaction of the "casual observer" to creative works.[19] The trier of fact ends up seeing or hearing the works at issue multiple times and deliberating over their similarities or differences in a less than casual manner. By contrast, if conducted the right way, surveys could more accurately sample the immediate impressions of onlookers and then report that information to the trier of fact.

Even if one believes that the aesthetic reaction of audience members is the right metric for evaluating infringement, there are prudential considerations when using surveys to gain insight into that reaction. Even the best survey that sheds light on how people respond to creative works cannot fully illuminate the complexities of this process. The concern here is that embracing survey evidence will somehow leave out critical parts of the aesthetic experience, potentially over- or under-protecting deserving creative works.[20] This objection deserves serious consideration and should help guide how surveys can be used to inform the substantial similarity analysis. Because our understanding of aesthetic reactions is far from perfect, survey evidence of those reactions should only serve as a supplement to the infringement analysis rather than the sole determinant.

Nevertheless, surveys of intended audiences should be permitted to aid in the substantial similarity determination. As noted in Chapter 3, copyright courts have been hostile to surveys, refusing to allow them into the infringement calculation at all. In the very few cases weighing the value of a proffered survey, there have been unfortunate mistakes in survey design. The surveys at issue queried respondents on the likelihood of confusing the defendant's work with the plaintiff's work, information more relevant for trademark infringement than copyright infringement.[21] These mistakes may not be the fault of clumsy survey designs, but rather stem from the relative difficulty in figuring out how to interrogate particular audiences on their aesthetic responses rather than their potential for confusion. After all, one cannot simply ask audience members if they think one copyrighted work is "substantially similar" to the other.

Yet it is not impossible to design a survey that is relevant to the substantial similarity analysis. Open-ended questions allowing a respondent to select a degree of similarity might do the trick. For example, members of the target audience could rate the works at issue on a five-point scale, with one standing for "not at all similar" and five for "very similar."[22] Surveys could also ask audiences to identify the components of a copyrighted work that they found most noticeable or enjoyable. Neuroimaging itself may offer valuable data for survey design, revealing which parts of the works at issue are potentially most salient to the relevant demographic.

Even if surveys offer incomplete information about audience thought, they would provide more inputs for appreciating audience mindsets, thereby prompting a salutary cognitive realignment. Today, we know little to nothing about how judges and juries arrive at their infringement determinations. Without guidance, people tend to evaluate scenarios from their own perspective.[23] It is likely that decision-makers in copyright cases are constantly failing to appreciate the perspective of relevant audiences, even on those few occasions when they are instructed by courts to adopt that perspective. They may need a legal nudge, in the form of survey evidence, to approach the substantial similarity analysis from a different, less solipsistic point of view.

Debiasing the Trier of Fact

In most areas of the law, we do not believe that the very act of setting boundaries on the mental calculations of the trier of fact, regardless of the content of those boundaries, renders those calculations unreliable. Jurors are not subatomic particles whose positions will inevitably be disturbed by the act of trying to locate those positions. Nevertheless, substantial similarity doctrine has long proceeded under just such a belief about the fragility of the trier of fact. Believing "that one could simply not reason about the aesthetic,"[24] courts have trodden extremely lightly, worrying that attempts to specify infringement will disturb jurors' mental calculations. If this agnostic approach to substantial similarity was once justified given the absence of information as to how audiences actually appreciate art, neuroscientific discoveries make the justification no longer tenable. The law is filled with mechanisms designed to debias and improve legal decision making. Copyright infringement should no longer be any different.

Neuroaesthetic research argues for one concrete doctrinal debiasing innovation: the trier of fact should evaluate substantial similarity *before* determining whether actual copying took place. A common complaint about the current infringement paradigm is that judges and juries are biased by whatever determination they make about whether copying occurred when deciding whether that copying is improper. Keep in mind that there are two separate steps to the infringement analysis. First, there must be a determination of whether copying took place. At this step, the trier of fact can be aided by expert testimony and may dissect the works into their component parts for comparison. Here, the decision is whether similarities are probative of copying, not whether that copying is substantial enough to be considered improper. Only after this first step is there a comparison of the target audience's aesthetic response to the two works – the substantial similarity analysis – an evaluation that currently precludes expert guidance or dissection.

The problem with the present ordering of these two separate stages of the infringement analysis is that the copying in fact step may skew the trier of fact's assessment of substantial similarity. The copying in fact analysis considers copying of either protectable or unprotectable expression as probative. The danger is that once any copying has been found, that initial finding will spill over into the separate question of whether this copying was improper. As one court noted, once a jury has been exposed to expert testimony on the separate issue of "copying in fact," it cannot "forget that evidence in analyzing the problem" of substantial similarity.[25]

A way to help with this problem is to reverse the order of the two analyses. The trier of fact should decide substantial similarity first. If there is a conclusion that the two works are substantially similar, then there can be an examination of copying in fact. Hence, if recreating audience aesthetic judgment is the touchstone for substantial similarity, then the jurors in the *Led Zeppelin* case should have been exposed to the relevant "Taurus" and "Stairway to Heaven" compositions quickly and then asked for their judgment as to substantial similarity. If they had concluded the two works were not substantially similar, then there would be no need to proceed to the separate question of copying in fact.

Although one might worry that this resequencing will cause the substantial similarity analysis to improperly influence the copying in fact test, this seems less likely than the reverse. Copying in fact is much more of a structured analysis than substantial similarity. It permits analytical dissection and expert testimony about which kinds of similarities should be considered probative. As a result, even when substantial similarity is found, this finding is unlikely to stampede the more bounded copying in fact analysis.

This idea about reordering the infringement decision has been suggested before.[26] It should be given even more serious consideration given the teachings of neuroaesthetics. In addition to serving a debiasing function, reversing the order of the two components of copyright infringement would better recreate the timing of aesthetic encounters. In an early formulation of the substantial similarity test, one court of appeals proposed a waiting period between the observer's experience of one work and her experience of another. The court described the test as inquiring whether an ordinary observer, "given an interval of two or three weeks between a casual reading of [plaintiff's] story and a similar uncritical view of [defendant's work]," would perceive the former in the latter.[27] Although this staggered reading of the two works proved too inefficient to implement, the motivating idea seems to be that the essence of creative works can best be ascertained through immediate experience with those works. Infringement should not be assessed by a labored comparison of one work to another, lest that creative essence somehow become overlooked or fade under the pressure of a more logical comparison. Better to engage in a fast, casual review in order to discern the work's aesthetic value. In general, courts fear that too much time with a work causes deliberation to trump instinct, making the observer's impression less probative of infringement. Neuroscientific research reveals that there is some truth to these judicial suppositions. Reversing the order of the two central infringement determinations would help facilitate a more accurate rendering of an audience's immediate impressions.

Different Aesthetic Approaches for Different Creative Media

If there was ever a doubt that audiences evaluate different artistic media in different ways, neuroscience has put those doubts to rest. Particular areas of the brain process, store, and retrieve music, but are not activated by other types of creative expression.[28] We tend to dissect musical works into their component parts while evaluating images holistically. This suggests that the common substantial similarity instruction that the trier of fact should assess whether two works have the same "look and feel" tracks actual audience experiences for some media but not others.

Neuroaesthetics tells us that the answer is not to stick with a universal approach to substantial similarity regardless of art form. Instead, expert testimony is needed to help the trier of fact understand which aspects of a work will be most salient to audiences depending on artistic medium. For example, an expert could provide the trier of fact with knowledge that, for music, the similarity of a particular segment to another should be more telling than in non-music cases. Given the scientific evidence, jurors should not be told to rely on "total sound effect" when determining substantial similarity in music copyright cases as they are today.[29]

Not every copyright case warrants expert testimony as to aesthetic reaction. Scientists have more insight into some kinds of aesthetic encounters than others, which should be reflected in the substantial similarity analysis. Perhaps unsurprisingly, abstract art prompts more varied aesthetic reactions than representational art.[30] Neuroscientists have had more success at isolating emotional reactions to musical works than other creative works.[31] This might mean that music cases or representational art cases can begin to utilize insights from neuroaesthetic studies whereas other infringement matters will need to wait until our understanding of the relevant aesthetic reaction improves. Given the findings of neuroaesthetic research, however, the current ban on all expert guidance in determining substantial similarity regardless of art form seems inappropriate.[32]

None of these suggested reforms would replace the current substantial similarity test. Not only are there significant limitations on what brain imaging technologies can detect when it comes to the complex neural processes involved in aesthetic judgment, but we know that psychology's influence on the law tends more to reform than revolution. Instead, as in other areas of the law, neuroscience seems ripe for making inroads in the infringement analysis without supplanting it. We understand the audiences for creative works much better than we could have even a few years ago. That understanding should be leveraged to rehabilitate our troubled system for determining copyright infringement.

Notes

[1] George Dickie, *Is Psychology Relevant to Aesthetics?*, 71 PHIL. REV. 285, 302 (1962).

[2] Blake Gopnik, *Aesthetic Science and Artistic Knowledge*, in AESTHETIC SCIENCE: CONNECTING MINDS, BRAINS, AND EXPERIENCE 129, 130 (A.P. Shinmamura & S.E. Palmer eds., 2012).

3   Bevil R. Conway & Alexander Rehding, *Neuroaesthetics and the Trouble with Beauty*, 11 PLOS BIOLOGY 1, 4 (2013).

4   PAUL M.W. HACKETT, PSYCHOLOGY AND PHILOSOPHY OF ABSTRACT ART: NEURO-AESTHETICS, PERCEPTION, AND COMPREHENSION (2016); Vered Aviv, *What Does the Brain Tell Us About Abstract Art?*, 8 FRONTIERS HUM. NEUROSCI. 85 (2014).

5   PAUL B. ARMSTRONG, HOW LITERATURE PLAYS WITH THE BRAIN: THE NEUROSCIENCE OF READING AND ART 20 (2013).

6   Shyamkrishna Balganesh, *The Normativity of Copying in Copyright Law*, 62 DUKE L.J. 203, 251–55 (2012).

7   Steven T. Lowe, *Death of Copyright 3: The Awakening*, 41 L.A. LAW. 28, 30 (2018).

8   Shyamkrishna Balganesh et al., *Judging Similarity*, 100 IOWA L. REV. 267, 281 (2014).

9   Robert Kirk Walker & Ben Depoorter, *Unavoidable Aesthetic Judgments in Copyright Law: A Community of Practice Standard*, 109 NW. U. L. REV. 343, 358–71 (2015); Alfred C. Yen, *Copyright Opinions and Aesthetic Theory*, 71 S. CAL. L. REV. 247 (1998).

10 Pamela Samuelson et al., *The Copyright Principles Project: Directions for Reform*, 25 BERKELEY TECH. L.J. 1175, 1209–13 (2010).

11 17 U.S.C. § 107.

12 Harper & Row, Pub., Inc. v. Nation Enters., 471 U.S. 539, 566 (1985).

13 Barton Beebe, *An Empirical Study of U.S. Copyright Fair Use Decisions, 1978–2005*, 156 U. PA. L. REV. 549, 617 (2008).

14 MARTIN SKLADANY, BIG COPYRIGHT VERSUS THE PEOPLE: HOW MAJOR CONTENT PROVIDERS ARE DESTROYING CREATIVITY AND HOW TO STOP THEM 3 (2018).

15 See Molly Shaffer Van Houweling, *Distributive Values in Copyright*, 83 TEX. L. REV. 1535, 1575 (2005).

16 Andrew Gilden, *Copyright's Market Gibberish*, 94 WASH. L. REV. 1019, 1081–82 (2019).

17 *Id.*

18 JESSICA SILBEY, THE EUREKA MYTH: CREATORS, INNOVATORS, AND EVERYDAY INTELLECTUAL PROPERTY 149–60 (2015).

19 Fulks v. Knowles-Carter, 207 F. Supp. 3d 274, 279 (S.D.N.Y. 2016); M & D Int'l Corp. v. Chan, 901 F. Supp. 1502, 1511 n.3 (D. Haw. 1995); United Feature Syndicate, Inc. v. Koons, 817 F. Supp. 370, 377 (S.D.N.Y. 1993).

20 There would also be concerns about the accuracy of such surveys, but there is no reason to think that judges, in their gatekeeping function, could not screen out unreliable surveys from probative ones, just as they do in other legal contexts.

21 See, for example, Ideal Toy Corp. v. Kenner Prods., 443 F. Supp. 291, 298–99, 304 (S.D.N.Y. 1977).

[22] Jamie Lund, *An Empirical Examination of the Lay Listener in Music Composition Copyright Infringement*, 11 VA. SPORTS & ENT. L.J. 137, 155 (2011).

[23] Jeanne C. Fromer & Mark A. Lemley, *The Audience in Intellectual Property Infringement*, 112 MICH. L. REV. 1251, 1283 (2014).

[24] Barton Beebe, Bleistein, *The Problem of Aesthetic Progress, and the Making of American Copyright Law*, 117 COLUM. L. REV. 319, 341 (2017).

[25] Whelan Assocs. v. Jaslow Dental Lab., Inc., 797 F.2d 1222, 1233 (3d Cir. 1986). See also Intervest Construction, Inc. v. Canterbury Estate Homes, Inc., 554 F.3d 919, 920 (11th Cir. 2008) (noting that even a "properly instructed" juror will have difficulty separating the copying-in-fact and substantial similarity analyses).

[26] Irina D. Manta, *Reasonable Copyright*, 53 B.C. L. REV. 1303, 1349–50 (2012).

[27] Harold Lloyd Corp. v. Witwer, 65 F.2d 1, 27 (9th Cir. 1933).

[28] OLIVER SACKS, MUSICOPHILIA: TALES OF MUSIC AND THE BRAIN 117–18 (2008); Margit Livingston & Joseph Urbinato, *Copyright Infringement of Music: Determining Whether What Sounds Alike Is Alike*, 15 VAND. J. ENT. & TECH. L. 227, 280 (2013).

[29] Arnstein v. Porter, 154 F.2d 464, 476 (2d Cir. 1946) (Clark, J., dissenting). See also Edwards v. Raymond, 22 F. Supp. 3d 293, 300–01 (S.D.N.Y. 2014) (evaluating substantial similarity of two musical works according to "total concept and overall feel").

[30] Edward A. Vessel et al., *Stronger Shared Taste for Natural Aesthetic Domains Than for Artifacts of Human Culture*, 179 COGNITION 121, 122 (2018).

[31] W. Tecumseh Fitch et al., *Bio-Aesthetics and the Aesthetic Trajectory: A Dynamic Cognitive and Cultural Perspective*, in NEUROAESTHETICS 59, 94 (Martin Skov & Oshin Vartanian eds., 2009).

[32] Allowing in expert testimony as to differences in artistic mediums will make it somewhat more difficult to accomplish my second suggestion of reordering the infringement analysis to try to get a truly immediate reaction from the trier of fact. Still, even under these conditions, expert testimony will facilitate a better understanding of audience reaction while still allowing more rapid assessments of aesthetic appeal than currently possible.

8 ADVERTISING, FAST AND SLOW

Just as neuroaesthetics can be enlisted to reform the law of copyright infringement, so may consumer neuroscience be used to revamp trademark law's distinctiveness, confusion, and dilution analyses. Neural proof of these consumer mental states will inevitably be submitted by trademark attorneys hoping to make their case, and the weight of such evidence is likely to alter the ways in which trademark infringement and dilution are determined. My hope is that these changes will not be accepted passively, but rather courts and legislators will reconsider what they mean by these legal terms as neuroscience begins to alter their character. The dominant rationale for trademark protection – the reduction of consumer search costs – is an inadequate normative guide for such a reconsideration. It offers no logical stopping point when determining the importance of small changes in consumer perception as revealed through fMRI and EEG readings. Here, I offer a different principle – focusing judicial attention on consumers' cognitive responses, not their emotional ones – to help steer trademark jurisprudence through a new technological chapter.

THE NEED FOR FIRST PRINCIPLES

As one psychologist notes in tracing the history of psychology and American law, "experts and their techniques are expensive and in the long run will do what will benefit whichever side commands the greatest resources."[1] This is a concern for all intellectual property regimes, but particularly for trademark law. Although gradually declining in cost, the techniques of neuroscience can be prohibitively expensive, leading to alliances between researchers and advertisers. It is no accident that one of the focal points in neuroscientific research is studying how to make famous trademarks even more important to consumer decision-making. It is well-established brands, not upstarts, that are devoting resources to run brain scans on prospective consumers.

What do the brands guiding consumer neuroscience research want for their money? Of course, they want to understand prospective shoppers better so they can engineer more effective sales pitches. But when neuroscientific evidence is introduced in court, these mark holders will want to reinforce a view of consumers as hurried and easily confused. This view of the consumer as a "moron in a hurry" makes it easier to win trademark infringement verdicts and stop rival businesses.[2] Whether use of a term is actually confusing to consumers or not, there is a strategic advantage for mark holders in engineering a generous definition of consumer confusion to limit the advertising activities of competitors.

The incentives also align with research that will make it easier to demonstrate mark distinctiveness and dilution. When speaking to non-legal audiences, neuromarketing specialists stress the importance of using trademark law to maintain legal control over aspects of the marketing environment discovered to have particular resonance in consumers' minds.[3] Businesses will want the law to make it easier for them to claim ownership of particular words, even when those words appear more descriptive of product characteristics than product source. They will also endorse research supporting a broader tarnishment doctrine, one that protects the emotional meanings engineered for their brands from more than just unauthorized sexualized uses.[4]

The story of psychologist-sponsored trademark surveys offers a cautionary example about the effects of scientific innovation on trademark law. Those surveys, first introduced in the early twentieth century, benefitted trademark holders by making confusion easier to prove. Psychological research of the time emphasized consumers' limited intellectual capabilities. Judges ended up trading earlier views of a cautious and logical consuming public for a description of that public as "that vast multitude which includes the ignorant, the unthinking and the credulous, who, in making purchases, do not stop to analyze, but are governed by appearances and general impressions."[5] These changes in legal doctrine, spurred by an embrace of the science of psychology, strengthened the hand of advertisers. By making it easier to assert trademark rights in merely descriptive terms and to demonstrate that consumers would be confused by alternate uses of those terms, courts turned trademarks into potent business resources, encouraging further investment in psychological techniques designed to burnish their emotional resonance with consumers.[6]

One might object that consumer neuroscience need not favor trademark plaintiffs and that courts can only go where the evidence takes them. But science is not value-neutral. Reading fMRI results requires interpretation, and there will be consequences from interpreting brain images one way instead of another. The concern is that judges and lawmakers may not appreciate this. Even those excited about integrating neuroscientific evidence with legal doctrine caution against an "fMRI fetishism" that causes adjudicators to be more persuaded by this evidence than warranted and to fail to consider the implications of neuroscientific evidence in light of the underlying justifications behind different legal regimes.[7]

Because history counsels that a "better" understanding of the brain means more evidence favorable to trademark holders, it is important that, from the outset, courts assess the influence of consumer neuroscientific evidence against a normative guide. Trademark law has a single dominant first principle: the reduction of consumer search costs. But this single principle is inadequate to assess the consequences of making it easier to prove mark distinctiveness, confusion, and dilution through neural imaging.

INADEQUACY OF THE SEARCH COSTS JUSTIFICATION

The elimination of search costs serves as the guiding justification for modern trademark law. The search costs theory goes like this. Unauthorized trademark usage forces consumers to spend valuable time and effort to scrutinize advertising representations. If I see an advertisement for a tablet computer featuring the "Apple" name yet coming from a different entity than the Cupertino, California-based electronics colossus, I have to waste my limited cognitive and temporal resources evaluating the advertisement more closely than I would otherwise. Even if I do not end up purchasing the product under the mistaken assumption that it comes from the Cupertino company, I will still have to scrutinize this commercial representation more heavily than if such an unauthorized use of the Apple mark was simply prohibited. Saving me from this wasted effort has become trademark law's prime directive. "It would be nearly impossible to overstate the extent to which the search costs theory now dominates as the theoretical justification of trademark law."[8]

If search costs are the primary lens for interpreting consumer neuroscience's entry into trademark law, some changes stemming from trademark law's impending neural turn appear salutary. Additional proof of acquired distinctiveness could help courts make more accurate judgments as to whether a word or symbol actually signals source to consumers. In this way, neuroscience might help reduce the danger of trademark false positives: trademark recognition for marks that do not actually indicate source. Such recognition threatens to block competitors from effectively communicating with consumers while doing little to ease shoppers' cognitive burdens.

Similarly, by focusing more attention on likelihood of confusion factors that could be tethered to neural data of consumer perception (like mark strength and actual confusion), neuroscience promises to better reconstruct consumer thought processes. That is arguably a good thing as well. A more accurate read of consumer confusion helps prevent unauthorized uses that send deceptive signals into the marketplace. From the search costs perspective, shoppers will be saved from spending unnecessary cognitive energy on carefully scrutinizing the origins of their prospective purchases.

Yet there are drawbacks to simply evaluating the implications of consumer neuroscience for trademark law according to the search costs model. At least at first, importing neuroscientific evidence into trademark law could create a trademark regime of haves and have nots. We have already seen a version of this with judicial presumptions against those who do not pay for survey evidence.[9] Although the costs of neural imaging are decreasing, they still represent a significant expense for would-be litigants. Smaller companies seeking to challenge the distinctiveness of a larger rival's mark or defending themselves from an infringement claim may be forced to capitulate rather than suffer the expense of hiring a competing neuroscientific expert. If search costs remain the lodestar for courts assessing trademark infringement, a desire to prevent any confusion among consumers may further tilt an already unequal playing field in favor of deep-pocketed companies that can marshal the resources for neuroscientific evidence purporting to lay bare those search costs.[10]

It is important to realize that there are different scenarios where consumers may be considered "confused" and not all of them should give rise to an action for trademark infringement. Confusion is not just an empirical question, but a normative one as well. The search costs justification offers no logical stopping point for a court trying to assess how much confusion is too much. For example, some courts have recognized claims for "initial interest confusion," whereby a consumer first perceives a product as coming from the plaintiff but then quickly recognizes that the product actually comes from the defendant.[11] Take the situation where a keyword search using a trademark on Google or Bing turns up a competitor's website instead of the trademark holder's, momentarily distracting the consumer before a purchase has been made. The courts have struggled with these scenarios, sometimes finding a legally-sufficient amount of confusion, even though the confusion quickly dissipates upon reaching the competitor's website and consumers arguably benefit from exposure to more product choices when competitors can use rival brands as keyword search terms.[12]

Today's neural readers can detect fleeting changes in blood flow that last less than a second. The question for courts will be if an evanescent detection of confusion should dictate a finding of infringement. As the financial backers of consumer neuroscience strive to uncover more and more precise measurements of consumer confusion in the laboratory, evidence showing momentary confusion will be available to courts deciding trademark cases. Under the search costs theory, such evidence would be compelling proof of infringement.

Along similar lines, the search costs theory has been mobilized to justify trademark dilution. According to some, consumers experience so-called "internal search costs" when a familiar brand name is presented in a new context.[13] Take the real-life case of one "Rolls Royce Rizzy," a rapper specializing in bawdy rhymes.[14] Consumers may not be confused such that they think the rapper formally partnered with the luxury car maker. But the disjunction between the rapper's use of the famous brand and the car maker's upper-crust reputation might cause a momentary double take – an "internal search cost" – inside their heads. Prior studies, not dependent on neuroscience, supposedly showed that dilutive uses of a famous brand name (e.g., DOGIVA dog treats and HEINEKEN popcorn) caused consumers to take a few hundred milliseconds longer to recall the famous brand than if they had never been exposed to the dilutive stimulus.[15] Perhaps such meager impacts on consumer recall should be considered insufficient to demonstrate a legally cognizable harm, particularly given the countervailing expressive interests of dilution defendants.[16] Under the search costs theory, however, one could argue that the consumer should be protected from even a few hundred milliseconds of cognitive consternation. These moments of consumer bewilderment will become easier to prove upon the admission of fMRI and EEG readings.

TWO SYSTEMS OF CONSUMER REASONING

If the search costs theory represents a flawed guide for navigating trademark law's impending collision with neuroscience, what should take its place? Trademark law is about regulating advertising. As the legal scholar Arthur Leff wrote forty years ago: "There is no 'whole story' that can be told about anything, especially anything as socially, economically, literarily, anthropologically, philosophically, legally, historically, and politically complex as advertising."[17] Taking Leff's comment to heart, my aim here is not to produce a new unified theory of trademark law to supplant the search costs model. Instead, my goal is a more modest one of suggesting a supplemental principle – reinforcing trademark law's traditional role of interrogating and encouraging cognitive, not emotional, reasoning – to aid courts wrestling with how to apply new evidence and understandings of human behavior to trademark doctrine.

Sometimes consumers think long and hard about a purchasing decision; sometimes they operate instinctually. Psychologists posit dual reasoning models, the most famous and influential of which comes from Nobel prize-winning psychologist Daniel Kahneman. According to Kahneman, there are two systems of thought that can be at play when making a decision. One is an automatic, intuitive, largely unconscious process that Kahneman labels System 1 reasoning. The other is a conscious, deliberate, rational weighing of costs and benefits he designates System 2 reasoning.[18]

One might describe System 1 as the emotional side of consumer choice and System 2 as the deliberative side.[19] System 1's instinctual decision-making can be extremely useful. We do not have the cognitive resources to engage in a lengthy, rational internal dialogue about every choice we make. Imagine using the laborious System 2 model for every buying decision, no matter how small or routine. But the automaticity of System 1 can also translate into exploitable flaws and biases that advertisers can use to place consumers at a disadvantage.[20]

Trademark law has traditionally focused its attention on System 2 reasoning even if it has not called it by that name. The law of trademarks polices the informational signals that consumers rely on to determine the source of products and services offered for sale. When reliable, these signals help consumers make cognitive decisions about the source of goods. Source indicators can be used to bring up memories of past experiences with the manufacturer and item at issue. They can also be used to find product reviews, whether from informal sources or institutions that test products. A trademark that serves as a source indicator can be used to access information released by government agencies (e.g., a product recall) or by competitors. All this information can be employed by the consumer to weigh the pros and cons of purchase.

Courts have tended to emphasize the dispassionate, rational side of decision-making in trademark decisions. This focus tends to train judicial attention on information used for rational choices rather than emotional instinct. Courts explain that "rational confusion" is the only kind of confusion that should be countenanced by trademark law.[21] For example, the reason a judge gave for holding a defendant's use of the Wal-Mart name and "smiley-face" marks non-infringing was that the defendant combined use of these trademarks with "unflattering words, images and portions of words that no rational consumer would expect Wal-Mart to associate with its own marks."[22]

This is not to say, of course, that there is not an emotional component to branding. As neuroscience has made clear, there is a lot more conveyed by the COKE trademark than the product's origin from the Atlanta, Georgia-based soft-drink company. Advertisers spend most of their efforts trying to impregnate trademark words and symbols with emotional meaning, not simply providing consumers with factual inputs for System 2 reasoning. Just think of all the attention marketers give to color choice and other visual cues, selections that contain little valuable information for System 2 decision-making.

Generally speaking, however, trademark law has avoided explicit consideration of the emotional impact of particular advertising strategies. The likelihood of confusion factors employ various inputs – like mark similarity and relatedness of the plaintiff's and defendant's product areas – to assess a consumer's rational perception of the source of the defendant's product. To the extent these factors could also be used to assess more emotional aspects of consumer decision-making, the courts have declined the invitation. For example, of all the likelihood of confusion factors, purchaser sophistication seems most suited to diagnosing when System 1 reasoning about commercial stimuli might be at play. The sophistication factor invites judicial assessments of a trademark's and shopping milieu's power to override deliberative faculties. Nevertheless, a comprehensive study revealed that a large percentage of infringement cases failed to address the factor at all.[23] Instead, there is a general judicial reluctance to designate any consumer group as more sophisticated than another, i.e., less susceptible to advertisers' emotional arts.[24]

Trademark law's historical reluctance to interrogate the System 1 thought processes of consumers may stem from prudential concerns. System 2 influences are easier to detect than influences on System 1 thinking since the latter act largely below the surface of conscious awareness. For example, the difficulty of demonstrating an "association" between the plaintiff's and defendant's marks necessary to make a case for dilution has limited the availability of that cause of action. Proof of this kind of spontaneous, unthinking mental process in consumers' heads has been hard to come by. By contrast, survey evidence of confusion seems to focus on System 2 cognition, assessing whether consumers deliberating over an advertising stimulus will mistake it for the plaintiff's trademark. As challenging as it is to get an accurate read of elements of conscious consumer perception (like the perceived similarity between two marks), evidence of unconscious consumer responses to trademarks has been even harder to obtain. As a result, trademark law's efforts to channel consumer perception have historically focused on cognitive rather than emotional decision-making.

Emotion is starting to play a larger role in trademark law, however. As described below, relatively recent changes to the law make consumers' emotional responses to advertising a focal point when assessing liability. These changes offer opportunities for consumer neuroscientists promising more information on consumers' emotional responses to advertising stimuli. Researchers studying consumer emotion claim to be able to avoid the problem of suggestive survey questions by simply "reading out" the brand personality traits that "exist in the mind of the consumer a priori."[25] These neural readings of brand personality promise measurement of consumers' emotional understanding and engagement with brands. If you believe the neuroscientists, the evidentiary barriers that caused courts to avoid consideration of shoppers' System 1 reasoning in the past will soon be overcome.

MOVING TOWARD EMOTION

More recent initiatives in trademark law are geared to assessing and regulating the emotional System 1 decisions made by consumers. Unlike an action for trademark infringement, an action for trademark dilution does not require proof that consumers will mistake the defendant's mark for the plaintiff's, making an incorrect assumption as they rationally evaluate whether or not to buy the defendant's product. Instead, dilution law stops unauthorized uses of famous trademarks that somehow dim the signaling power of the famous trademark on a non-cognitive, subconscious, emotional level.[26] A successful dilution by tarnishment claim rests on the notion that consumers irrationally lower their estimation of the plaintiff's famous trademark when they see the defendant use that mark in a different, non-confusing context. An instinctual downgrading of the Rolls-Royce automotive brand after seeing another actor use that brand in a non-confusing but sexualized context is System 1 reasoning, not System 2 deliberation.[27] Until the arrival of a federal cause of action for dilution in 1995, courts rarely countenanced this kind of emotional reasoning on the part of consumers.[28]

Courts have also recognized a doctrine of "post-sale" confusion that occurs not at the moment of purchase, but when onlookers see a purchaser brandishing a trademarked item and wrongly associate the item with the plaintiff's mark.[29] At first glance, the theory behind post-sale confusion might seem to concern itself only with consumers' System 2 deliberations. One justification for policing post-sale confusion is to protect downstream purchasers making their own decisions about products. The initial purchasers of a counterfeit Rolex watch may know exactly what they are getting given the low cost and circumstances of the watch's purchase. But onlookers seeing the counterfeit may not. They may wrongly attribute any defects in product quality to the actual trademark owner instead of the counterfeiter. Under this rationale, the doctrine of post-sale confusion helps prevent misleading information from polluting the rational decision-making of potential future purchasers.

Yet the evidence of such misleading information influencing downstream purchasing decisions is often quite thin. The narrative of the confused onlooker is plausible, but it may be just as likely that onlookers recognize the counterfeit good for what it is and experience no confusion as to source. If a frugal friend suddenly starts sporting a Rolex watch, we will likely doubt its provenance.

Perhaps recognizing this evidentiary deficit, courts articulate an alternative justification for post-sale confusion that has little to do with consumer confusion as to source at all. Instead, they assert the doctrine's necessity as a means to regulate consumers' emotional attitudes toward a brand. According to some scholars, the doctrine of post-sale confusion is really a pretext for a larger concern with preserving the ability of luxury goods to signal status.[30] They point to judges openly reasoning that past purchasers of the trademark owners' branded goods will suffer if they witness others displaying the same mark on unauthorized products.[31]

For example, in one case involving the sale of kit cars that resembled Ferraris, the court observed: "If the country is populated with hundreds, if not thousands, of replicas of rare, distinct, and unique vintage cars, obviously they are no longer unique. Even if a person seeing one of these replicas driving down the road is not confused, Ferrari's exclusive association with this design has been diluted and eroded."[32] Note that this description of post-sale confusion really describes a harm to the emotional power of the Ferrari brand built up through advertising. The Ferrari name signals status and prestige, but these emotional valences come under threat when Ferrari luxury suddenly seems accessible to a larger swath of the population. Actual Ferrari cars mechanically perform just as well as they ever did, but consumers' emotional response to the Ferrari brand changes if it no longer indicates exclusivity. Under this rationale, courts recognize post-sale confusion to preserve the emotional snob appeal of the mark, not to prevent buyers from making rational decisions under false pretenses.[33] Like dilution law, post-sale confusion appears geared less to consumers' rational consideration of product information and more to protecting the investment made by famous brand holders in acquiring emotional mindshare.

The arrival of neuroscientific evidence of consumer thought may offer legally cognizable evidence of how the buying public emotionally responds to different trademarks. A change in a trademark's neural signature after consumers are exposed to knock-off products might be offered to illustrate the harms of post-sale confusion. Dilution by tarnishment claims could be bolstered by showing how various indices in a mark's neural map (e.g., its reputation for ruggedness) decline once consumers have been exposed to the defendant's mark. Even though inquiries into System 1 reasoning have traditionally been disdained or avoided by trademark courts, this may change as such reasoning suddenly appears susceptible to measurement, not judicial speculation. With neuroscience, the practical barriers that once restrained courts from exploring the emotional aspects of consumer decision-making may no longer seem to be an issue.

PRIVILEGING DELIBERATION OVER EMOTION

A move to legally recognize consumers' emotional reactions toward brands is not necessarily in consumers' best interests. Recognizing evidence of emotional value in a trademark is likely to privilege that value. In determining how neuroscientific insights should be incorporated into trademark law, courts should try to limit themselves to consideration of consumers' cognitive, deliberative judgments, not their emotional, instinctual ones. At the very least, courts should exercise an abundance of caution as businesses clamor to introduce neural information of consumer emotional state.

It would be fair to ask why trademark law should limit itself to only one side of consumers' dual reasoning system, particularly when laboratory discoveries are shedding new light on the role of emotions in human decision-making. More accurate understanding of consumer perception represents a longstanding goal for judges deciding trademark cases. Discounting neural evidence of automatic, emotional reasoning would seem to ignore that goal just as it begins to come within reach.[34] Nevertheless, there are at least three good reasons for limiting trademark law's ambit to the System 2 side of consumer decision-making.

First, even as neuroscience offers evidence of emotional response, it should be kept in mind that emotions represent complex mental processes that are not yet fully understood by researchers. Neuroscientists are on safer ground when they map the neural indices of familiarity with a brand – evidence directly relevant to trademark law's acquired distinctiveness analysis – or visual similarity, which is important in determining likelihood of confusion. Trying to pinpoint the emotional response necessary to prove harm to a trademark's reputation requires consideration of many more variables. Given this complexity, allowing neuroscientific evidence of consumer emotion to decide trademark dilution cases could lead to anti-competitive outcomes.

For example, I may be familiar with the DUNKIN' mark for doughnuts and coffee and this familiarity may even be revealed through fMRI readings thereby supplying evidence correlated with acquired distinctiveness. But arguing that I have a particular positive emotional reaction to the DUNKIN' trademark that will be eroded by a non-confusing use of "Dunkin" on another product requires disentangling my general love of doughnuts with my specific feelings toward the DUNKIN' brand. The concern is treating neural evidence of an emotional reaction to a product as proof of an emotional attachment to a single trademark. More broadly, there is a danger in being overly persuaded by fMRI images that supposedly reveal the neural architecture of a complex, ill-defined emotional state like "tarnishment." As a prominent critic of brain imaging research warned years ago, neuroscientific examinations of concepts (whether psychological or legal) that are vague and unspecified naturally produce unreliable results.[35]

Courts should be extremely reluctant to recognize neuroscientific evidence of the psychological pull of a brand on the public that overlaps to any degree with the emotional hold of the product being sold under that brand. Because dilution law does not require that speech be misleading, it endangers a whole range of valuable expression in a way that infringement law does not. The danger of stifling this expression looms even larger if courts entertain neuroscientific evidence of trademark dilution that really reflects harm to entire product categories instead of particular trademarks.

Second, there are benefits to defining trademark law so as to prompt consumers to use their deliberative faculties instead of their automatic, instinctual ones. Trademark doctrines that allow some amount of confusion to exist actually benefit consumers by encouraging them to develop greater brand literacy and awareness. Consumers that experience confusion become better at distinguishing between trademarks; those lacking this experience fail to recognize important distinctions. Although many of our shopping decisions rely on the automaticity of System 1, we need moments of temporary confusion to slow the process down and engage System 2 to create new strategies for decoding advertising stimuli. Eventually, these new strategies may become so routine as to be automated and used by System 1 but we need System 2 reasoning to create them in the first place. "At the very least," intellectual property scholar Alfred Yen says, "modest confusion concerning trademarks actually helps consumers avoid confusion by helping them develop valuable cognitive skills that make distinguishing and understanding trademarks possible."[36]

Just as an overly broad view of consumer confusion threatens the development of these cognitive skills, an embrace of neuroscientific evidence of emotional response to trademarks could jeopardize consumers' ability to learn from and avoid advertising's emotional traps. Businesses spend an enormous amount of resources trying to convince us of a trademark's particular emotional meaning. Some attack this entire process as economically wasteful, with the money devoted to persuasive (as opposed to informational) advertising better spent on the research needed to make functionally better products.[37] But one doesn't have to be such an advertising skeptic to recognize that consumers need to develop the ability to comprehend and resist some of the emotional appeals engineered by advertisers. Just taking Apple's word for it that it "thinks differently" than other technology companies or uncritically accepting Ford's suggestion that its trucks are "Built Ford Tough" would lead to suboptimal choices in the marketplace. Laws like dilution that limit challenges to these emotional messages give consumers less practice in deciphering and resisting advertising's System 1 appeals. The consumer's affective response to the ROLLS ROYCE mark becomes less discerning if she never had the opportunity to be exposed to Rolls Royce Rizzy's slightly alternative take. Using neuroscientific evidence of changes to a mark's emotional meaning to prohibit alternative brand messages would hamper consumers' ability to develop greater literacy with the emotional language of modern advertising.

Finally, although my focus has been on courts' use of neuroscientific evidence and not advertisers' applied use of neuroscientific insights, the two are related. Trademark law rewards some advertising strategies while penalizing others. Even if neural imaging promises a way to more accurately predict consumer perception, and thereby makes it easier to detect consumer confusion and mark dilution, judges should address the difficult underlying question of which advertising strategies trademark law should be in the business of promoting and which ones it should undermine, or at least not reinforce, in furtherance of consumer welfare. Decisions about the admissibility and effect of consumer neuroscience evidence require courts to decide whether they should passively ratify advertising strategies that leverage the automatic, emotional side of human reasoning or more actively question the net social benefit of legal protection for such strategies.

For most of its history, trademark law has reacted passively to changing marketing methods instead of proactively shaping the ways in which consumers shop and producers sell. For example, the likelihood of confusion analysis adjusted to new forms of brand merchandizing (think John Deere key chains and t-shirts) by simply enlarging the sphere of potential confusion without really interrogating whether such merchandizing should be part of trademark law's remit. It is by no means clear that trademark holders should have exclusive rights over the sale of products that use marks primarily for their ornamental value, rather than as indicators of source. Nevertheless, a series of trademark infringement decisions in the 1970s and 1980s quickly ratified the right to use trademarks to merchandize.[38]

A historical counterexample offers a useful reference point for courts evaluating the proper role of consumer neuroscience evidence for trademark law. According to its originator, dilution law was designed to safeguard the "psychological hold" that successful advertising had on the public.[39] But courts were hesitant to enforce laws that provided businesses this power, which they considered a "radical" expansion.[40] Even though the whole point of the new dilution law was to arm mark holders with a way to stop non-confusing unauthorized uses of their marks, judges decided to require confusion for a successful dilution action. Other courts required proof of "actual dilution," evidence that was extremely hard to come by and not required by the statutory language. Part of this judicial resistance stemmed from a belief that dilution threatened a sort of mind control, with the law preventing consumers from shaking their initial impression of a famous mark. Out of antipathy to the very conception of dilution, courts made dilution impossible to prove.

The initial period of judicial intransigence to dilution law is instructive.[41] Resistance to dilution law came in the context of a larger social and legal backlash against 1950s advertising techniques that purported to rely on subliminal messaging and psychoanalysis to influence consumers. Federal officials and agencies and quasi-public regulators all reacted to put limits on these techniques because they appeared to violate an accepted vision of human autonomy.

Somewhat similarly, judges saw a stark difference between the traditional role of trademark law in regulating the deliberative, cognitive choices of consumers and its newer role in applying anti-dilution concepts to shape their unconscious, emotional thoughts. This fault line will be relevant again as courts confront neuroscientific evidence of a mark's unique emotional signature in consumers' minds. Any technology that promises to lay bare consumer thought processes will be enormously appealing to legal actors, but these actors also need to bear in mind the value in continuing to leave some effects of commercial speech outside of the scope of trademark protection.[42]

Notes

[1] Craig Haney, *Psychology and Legal Change: On the Limits of a Factual Jurisprudence*, 4 LAW & HUM. BEHAV. 147, 154 (1980).

[2] Morning Star Coop. Soc'y Ltd. v. Express Newspapers Ltd. I, [1979], EWHC (Ch) 113 [117] (Eng.).

[3] PATRICK M. GEORGES ET AL., NEUROMARKETING IN ACTION: HOW TO TALK AND SELL TO THE BRAIN 91 (2013).

[4] Take, for example, A.K. PRADEEP, THE BUYING BRAIN: SECRETS FOR SELLING TO THE SUBCONSCIOUS MIND 123 (2010).

[5] Florence Mfg. Co. v. J.C. Dowd & Co., 178 F. 73, 75 (2d Cir. 1910).

[6] MARK BARTHOLOMEW, ADCREEP: THE CASE AGAINST MODERN MARKETING 111 (2017).

[7] Francis X. Shen, *Law and Neuroscience 2.0*, 48 ARIZ. ST. L.J. 1043, 1051 (2016). *See also* David P. McCabe & Alan D. Castel, *Seeing Is Believing: The Effect of Brain Images on Judgments of Scientific Reasoning*, 107 COGNITION 343, 350–52 (2008) (showing that brain scans can cause potential jurors to accept flawed explanations of mental phenomena).

[8] Mark P. McKenna, *A Consumer Decision-Making Theory of Trademark Law*, 98 VA. L. REV. 67, 75 (2012).

[9] 2 J. THOMAS MCCARTHY, MCCARTHY ON TRADEMARKS § 12:14 (5th ed. 2021).

[10] Eventually, the costs of neuroscientific testing of consumers will likely come down, allowing different kinds of market actors to take advantage of fMRI and EEG readings. At that point, however, precedents friendly to famous brand holders may be cemented into place. See Oona A. Hathaway, *Path Dependence in the Law: The Course and Pattern of Legal Change in a Common Law System*, 86 IOWA L. REV. 601, 638 (2001).

[11] See, for example, Australian Gold, Inc. v. Hatfield, 436 F.3d 1228, 1239 (10th Cir. 2006).

[12] Nissan Motor Co. v. Nissan Computer Corp., 378 F.3d 1002, 1018 (9th Cir. 2004); Brookfield Commc'ns, Inc. v. W. Coast Entm't Corp. 174 F.3d 1036, 1061–65 (9th Cir. 1999). This is not to say that courts evaluating search costs never balance these costs against competing interests. Sometimes even when a defendant's activity momentarily confuses consumers, a judge will acknowledge that expressive concerns or competitive

harms, on balance, are more important than shopper efficiency. Lamparello v. Falwell, 420 F.3d 309, 315–18 (4th Cir. 2005). The problem is that trademark law offers little in the way of a developed framework for weighing these competing interests, making it all too easy for search costs to take center stage in the judicial imagination.

[13] WILLIAM LANDES & RICHARD POSNER, THE ECONOMIC STRUCTURE OF INTELLECTUAL PROPERTY LAW 168, 207 (2003); Jacob Jacoby, *The Psychological Foundations of Trademark Law: Secondary Meaning, Genericism, Fame, Confusion and Dilution*, 91 TRADEMARK REP. 1013, 1047 (2001).

[14] Rolls-Royce Motor Cars v. Robert D. Davis, No. 15-0417, slip op. at 15–16 (D.N.J. March 11, 2016).

[15] Maureen Morrin & Jacob Jacoby, *Trademark Dilution: Empirical Measures for an Elusive Concept*, 19 J. PUB. POL'Y & MKTG. 265 (2000).

[16] Recent scholarship questions the validity of these earlier dilution studies. Barton Beebe et al., *Testing for Trademark Dilution in Court and the Lab*, 86 U. CHI. L. REV. 611 (2019).

[17] ARTHUR LEFF, SWINDLING AND SELLING 148 (1976).

[18] DANIEL KAHNEMAN, THINKING, FAST AND SLOW 13 (2011).

[19] Jonathan St. B.T. Evans, *Dual Processing Account of Reasoning, Judgment, and Social Cognition*, 59 ANN. REV. PSYCHOL. 255, 256–57 (2008).

[20] Shmuel L. Becher & Yuval Feldman, *Manipulating, Fast and Slow: The Law of Non-Verbal Market Manipulations*, 38 CARDOZO L. REV. 459, 470–71 (2016); Jon D. Hanson & Douglas A. Kysar, *Taking Behaviorialism Seriously: The Problem of Market Manipulation*, 74 N.Y.U. L. REV. 630, 743 (1999).

[21] Pernod Ricard USA v. Bacardi USA, Inc., 653 F.3d 241, 252 n.12 (3d Cir. 2011).

[22] Smith v. Wal-Mart Stores, Inc., 537 F. Supp. 2d 1302, 1336 (N.D. Ga. 2008).

[23] Barton Beebe, *An Empirical Study of the Multifactor Tests for Trademark Infringement*, 94 CALIF. L. REV. 1581, 1642 (2006).

[24] See Incredible Technologies, Inc. v. Virtual Technologies, Inc., 400 F.3d 1007, 1016 (7th Cir. 2005).

[25] Yu-Ping Chen et al., *From "Where" to "What": Distributed Representations of Brand Associations in the Human Brain*, 52 J. MKTG. RES. 453, 455 (2015).

[26] Katya Assaf, *Brand Fetishism*, 43 CONN. L. REV. 83, 129 (2010); Gideon Parchomovsky & Alex Stein, *Intellectual Property Defenses*, 113 COLUM. L. REV. 1483, 1508 (2013).

[27] The court based its decision that the rapper's stage name tarnished the luxury car brand, in part, on the rapper's use of song titles like "Hoe in You" and an advertisement featuring "a scantily-clad woman."

[28] Even with the new federal law, courts were reluctant to accept the implications of protecting a trademark's emotional appeal from non-confusing marketing. They interpreted the statute in ways that rendered it ineffective, though this eventually changed after Congress revised the statute in 2006 to specifically address judicial intransigence. Mark Bartholomew, *Advertising and the Transformation of Trademark Law*, 38 N.M. L. REV. 1, 36–38 (2008). Some state legislatures had enacted their own dilution laws before the passage of the federal law, but judges were loath to enforce these as well. Sara Stadler Nelson, *The Wages of Ubiquity in Trademark Law*, 88 IOWA L. REV. 731, 763 (2003).

[29] Payless Shoesource, Inc. v. Reebok Int'l, Ltd., 998 F.2d 985, 989 (Fed. Cir. 1993); Louis Vuitton Malletier S.A. v. Sunny Merchandise Corp., 97 F. Supp. 3d 485 (S.D.N.Y. 2015).

[30] Mark P. McKenna, *Probabilistic Knowledge of Third-Party Trademark Infringement*, 2011 STAN. TECH. L. REV. 10, 12.

[31] Gen. Motors Corp. v. Keystone Auto. Indus., Inc., 453 F.3d 351, 358 (6th Cir. 2006); Acad. of Motion Picture Arts & Scis. v. Creative House Promotions, Inc., 944 F.2d 1446, 1457 (9th Cir. 1991).

[32] Ferrari S.P.A. Ecercizio Fabriche Automobili e Corse v. McBurnie, 11 U.S.P.Q.2d 1843, 1848 (S.D. Cal. 1989).

[33] This is not to say that a concern with maintaining one's status through the conspicuous display of certain material goods is completely irrational. But such a concern is more likely to be fueled by emotional considerations when compared to other criteria for purchase like product performance and reliability. Moreover, consumption based on the desire for status is correlated with lower life satisfaction, perhaps testifying to the irrational nature of some status-related consumer decision-making. *See* TIM KASSER, THE HIGH PRICE OF MATERIALISM 5–22 (2002).

[34] Scientists are still probing the truth of the split between emotional and cognitive thinking. Some psychological studies challenge the dual processing model favored by Kahneman and others, and even Kahneman admits to some overlap between System 1 and System 2. Yet some neuroscientists point to imaging results that they say affirm the presence of two different systems of consumer decision-making – one evaluative and goal-directed, the other automatic and habit-based. John P. O'Doherty et al., *Learning, Reward, and Decision Making*, 68 ANN. REV. PSYCH. 73 (2017); Antonio Rangel et al., *A Framework for Studying the Neurobiology of Value-Based Decision Making*, 9 NATURE REVS. NEUROSCI. 545, 547–48 (2008). My suggestion that trademark courts limit themselves to investigating System 2 reasoning does not depend on the empirical truth of the dual processing model, however, or the complete separation of one processing track from another. Even if these decision-making processes are not neurally discrete and consumers employ both System 1 and System 2 reasoning when making most or even all

purchasing decisions, there are normative reasons for courts in the trademark law context to focus on evidence of System 2 reasoning.

[35] WILLIAM R. UTTAL, THE NEW PHRENOLOGY: THE LIMITS OF LOCALIZING COGNITIVE PROCESSES IN THE BRAIN 21–22 (2001).

[36] Alfred C. Yen, *The Constructive Role of Confusion in Trademark*, 93 N.C. L. REV. 77, 125–26 (2014).

[37] Ralph S. Brown, Jr., *Advertising and the Public Interest: Legal Protection of Trade Symbols*, 57 YALE L.J. 1165, 1169 (1948).

[38] Stacey L. Dogan & Mark A. Lemley, *The Merchandising Right: Fragile Theory or Fait Accompli?*, 54 EMORY L.J. 461, 463–64 (2005).

[39] Frank I. Schechter, *The Rational Basis of Trademark Protection*, 40 HARV. L. REV. 813, 825 (1927).

[40] Nelson, *supra*, at 763.

[41] Over time, trademark holders overcame the initial judicial resistance to dilution law. In 2003, the US Supreme Court held that "actual dilution" needed to be proven for a successful dilution claim. Moseley v. V Secret Catalogue, 537 U.S. 418 (2003). Concerned that a requirement that plaintiffs prove actual dilution would effectively eviscerate the dilution cause of action, Congress quickly moved to pass a new law affirming that only a "likelihood of dilution" was required for a successful dilution claim and courts had no choice but to acquiesce.

[42] One might argue that if trademark law should not facilitate consumers' System 1 reasoning, then dilution law should be abandoned as a whole. At this point, however, dilution law does not seem to be going away. As discussed earlier, any legal changes prompted by consumer neuroscience are unlikely to include the abandonment of an entire cause of action.

CONCLUSION

Artists, audiences, judges. These are the three demographic categories that intellectual property law concerns itself with. The thought patterns of creators determine whether art and commercial design can enjoy legal protection from copyists. The boundaries of that protection are set according to audience perspectives on aesthetic appeal and consumer confusion. The law imagines artists to be more impetuous than deliberate, more holistic than detail-oriented.

Meanwhile, according to copyright law, the aesthetic reactions of audiences are impervious to outside study while simultaneously uniform across different groups and different artistic media. Design patent law presumes an audience that aesthetically prefers innovation in the look and feel of consumer goods. Trademark law acknowledges that audiences for commercial advertising remain somewhat out of touch with their own mental processing of trade symbols, but maintains that there is little recourse but to reconstruct that mental processing through judicial best guesses and surveys dependent on flawed self-reports. As we have learned, the neuroscientific research of the past two decades clashes with these legal constructions of artist and audience mentalities.

As for judges themselves, their predominate mental state might be described as insecurity. Aware that their formulation of artist and audience mindsets lacks empirical grounding, they fret over the accuracy of their hunches about the thoughts of the creative class and the average audience member. They resort to a kind of folk psychology, assuming that experiences with art and artistry must remain impenetrable to outsiders. They display similar discomfort in trying to reach into the minds of shoppers to determine when a commercial symbol successfully signals source or when one such symbol might be mistaken for another. Questioning their ability to comprehend human experiences with art and advertising, they long for better tools to diagnose relevant mental states of creators and their audiences.

Perhaps those tools are finally here, but their adoption by legal decision-makers is not inevitable. In a way, much of intellectual property law and the law in general remains attached to a belief in mind–body dualism. According to René Descartes and other dualist philosophers, instead of being anchored in the physical, the mind operates in its own non-physical plane. To the extent the legal system attaches rights and liabilities to particular mental states, the dualist view counsels skepticism as to materialist influences on behavior, preferring an account focusing on an ethereal, non-corporeal seat of responsibility in human consciousness.[1] By following the dualist view, and largely refusing to interrogate the minds of artists and audiences, intellectual property law has permitted hazy, indeterminate approaches to concepts like "creativity" and "similarity" to become settled doctrine.

Neuroscience tells us that all psychological states operate in the realm of the physical. It pushes against the dualist account, revealing that mental phenomena once considered non-physical, like a viewer's subjective experiences or the construction of mental imagery, can be traced through movements of blood and electrical impulses in the brain.

This does not mean that everything about human thought can be reduced to what goes on in the brain. Dualism is not completely dead – the abstract subjects we think about are not the same as the neural activity involved in thinking about them. Nevertheless, knowing more about the chemical and biological mechanics of thinking about these subjects offers new information about human capabilities. As our understanding of this physical realm grows, there is less reason to posit the unknowable nature of artistic production, aesthetic appreciation, and consumer perception of trade symbols. Some neuroaesthetic research contradicts the armchair psychology currently applied by the courts, as with the revelation that creativity relies on the same mental processes whether in the service of science or the arts. Other findings support generally held intuitions that have not yet found their way into legal doctrine, as with the confirmation that familiarity strongly influences aesthetic preference. Even if Holmes and other jurists of the past century were right that the mysteries of artistic creation and appreciation were too impenetrable to supply concrete criteria for those deciding intellectual property disputes, neuroscience now challenges the proposition that these mental phenomena must remain forever quarantined from meaningful legal determination.

Of course, it is not as straightforward as simply applying our growing knowledge of the physical to update intellectual property law. Judges set the terms of the interface between science and law, and there is much more to this interface than mere scientific merit. Concerns over judicial discretion and economy may cause some to prefer the status quo and resist the application of neuroscientific insights to intellectual property law. Even as it fills in some gaps of our understanding, application of neuroscientific teaching requires the drawing of new, difficult legal lines. For example, if one takes seriously this book's contention that the creativity threshold for copyright and design patents can and should be raised through broader consideration of prior art and artistic motivation, then legal decision-makers will need to spend more time assessing creativity than they do now. If there is one virtue of the current extremely low creativity threshold, it is that it does not consume much in the way of judicial resources. Hence, instead of making intellectual property a more manageable legal area, better understanding of the biology of human thought forces fundamental reexamination of the goals of copyright, patent, and trademark law and the doctrinal edifices constructed for realizing those goals.

Still, my hope is that legal decision-makers do choose to learn from neuroscience's study of art, design, and advertising and this reexamination is allowed to proceed. Although sometimes described as opposites,[2] the legal system and the sciences share a common purpose when it comes to better understanding of artists and audiences. Our system of intellectual property law is designed to foster social artifacts that allow for self-discovery. The subject matter of copyright, patent, and trademark law involves the cultural materials we use to express what makes us unique as well as what binds us to others. Artists manipulate paint, clay, and computer code to describe something about their surroundings. Even advertising – a cultural material we often try to avoid – serves as raw material for expressions and investigations of group belonging and difference. In describing the creative process,

James Baldwin wrote that "the conquest of the physical world is not man's only duty. He is also enjoined to conquer the great wilderness of himself. The precise role of the artist, then, is to illuminate that darkness."[3] A relentless, never satisfied sense of inquiry is at the heart of the intellectual creations meant to be encouraged by intellectual property law.

Neuroscientists also act as cartographers of Baldwin's "great wilderness." The brain, described as "the most complex object in the known universe," truly is a relatively unmapped and wild territory for human exploration.[4] Despite technological advances enabling increasingly precise imaging of brain activity, neuroscientists are still in search of principles that can explain all areas of brain function. Yet perfect understanding is not necessary for neuroscience to be relevant; partial discoveries can be celebrated and built on. By investigating the physical mechanics of creative activity and appreciation, neuroscientists cause us to question why we are the way we are. Neuroscience cannot tell us everything about what it means to be human, but it can tell us more about the human condition. This information, as best as it can given the limitations of both scientific and legal understanding, should be applied to light the way of artists and audiences in their lonely journeys.

Notes

[1] For a general discussion of mind–body dualism in US law, see Dov Fox & Alex Stein, *Dualism and Doctrine*, 90 IND. L.J. 975 (2015).

[2] C. P. SNOW, THE TWO CULTURES (Canto ed. 1998); Peter Lee, *Patent Law and the Two Cultures*, 120 YALE L.J. 2 (2010).

[3] James Baldwin, *The Creative Process, in* THE PRICE OF THE TICKET: COLLECTED NONFICTION, 1948–1985, at 315, 316 (1985).

[4] MATTHEW COBB, THE IDEA OF THE BRAIN: THE PAST AND FUTURE OF NEUROSCIENCE 7 (2020).

INDEX

191